Rothkranz Publishing

ISBN: 978-0-9909350-1-8

© 3rd printing 2019 Cara Brotman and Markus Rothkranz

Art and Photography by Markus Rothkranz

Most Recipes by Cara Brotman and some by Markus Rothkranz

Legal disclaimer: All information material contained herein is provided for general information purposes only. The information and material provided is not intended to diagnose or treat any condition or symptom and its use is not intended to be substitute for the medical or professional advice of a physician. The authors of this book are not responsible for any direct, indirect, special, punitive, incidental or consequential damages whatsoever from the use of the information and material herein, including without limitation, personal injury, illness, wrongful death, or any other personal or pecuniary loss.

LOVE ON A PLATE
The Gourmet Uncookbook

By Cara Brotman and Markus Rothkranz

3rd Printing

Contents

Introduction by Markus 8

Introduction by Cara 10

The Basics... 13

Things to Always Have Around 14

Flipping things over when drying... 16

BASIC ELEMENTS 17

Cashew Vanilla milk, Savory Cream, Sweet Cream.......................... 18

Sea moss... 20

Almond Cheese 22

Garlic Naan... 24

Lunch Meat, Cheese and Chips 26

Burger Patty.. 28

Mustard, Mayonaise, Relish, Ketchup....................................30

Creamy Mashed Potatoes, Veggies & Onion Rings...........................32

unMeat / Bacon / Jerky... 34

Fruit Cracker, Chocolate Syrup 36

DRINKS 38

Green Smoothie 40

Strawberry Smoothie 42

Cactus Aloe Smoothie 44

Raspberry Mint Lime cocktail 46

Grapefruit Garlic Ginger Daydream 48

Veggie Juice 50

Gourmet Chocolate milk 52

Green Dream Juice, Lemongrass Ginger Chuenchai 54

Pumpkin Parfait, Strawberry Parfait..56

Chocolate Smoothie 58

Pina Colada 60

SOUPS 62

Bangkok Thai Soup 64

Unchicken Noodle Soup 66

Corn Chowder Soup 68

SALADS 70

Markus Basic Kale Salad 72

unCheese, Date, Pineapple Salad 74

Greek Salad 76

Green Crunch Salad 78

Asian Salad 80

Seaweed Salad 82

Tabouli Salad 84

SNACKS 86

Almond Nut Crunch 88

Freezer Chocolate, Marzipan 90

Dried Tomato poppers with cheese and tiny onion rings.....................92

Real Potato Chips...94

Various Chips for Dips 96

Chocolate Almond Flax Cookies 98

Orange Slices with Protein Powder 100

Chocolate-Dipped Almond Cookies 102

Apple Raviolis 104

Fruit Cracker 106

Brotwurst spreadable sausage substitute.................................108

APPETIZERS 110

Endive Hummus Boats 112

Spring Rolls 114

Jalapeño Poppers...116

BREAKFAST 118

unBacon, unEggs, Breakfast Sausage, Hash Browns, Pancakes...... 120

Fruit Salads 122

Oatmeal..124

Breakfast Crisps with Cashew Butter, Mango, Banana.....................126

Curry Omelet 128

Durian Custard with Fruit..130

Cleansing Breakfast..132

LUNCH 134

unTuna Salad., Mayonnaise...136

unChicken Tacos...138

Pumpkin Raviolis 140

Naan Wrap, Coconut Wrap 142

Rueben 144

DINNER 146

Kung Pao unChicken...148

Indian Feast 150

Spicy Thai Curry Noodle unChicken..152

Pasta in Cream Sauce 154

Spicy Thai Cabbage 156

Mango Blueberry Mint... 158

Pasta Pomodoro 160

Thai Curry Noodles.. 162

Tropical Salsa... 164

Gourmet Pizza.. 166

Vegetables Vesuvio over Noodles... 168

Barley on the Half shell... 170

Shitake Mushroom Pizza... 172

Sushi Nori.. 174

Sushi lite... 176

Nigiri... 178

Lasagna.. 180

Markus Pizza.. 182

KIDS   186

Macaroni and Cheese 188

Pop Tarts.. 190

Spaghettios..192

Broccoli and Cheese.. 194

DESSERTS   196

Crème Brûlée...198

Chocolate Tacos..200

90 Second Chocolate Ice Cream 202

Canoli... 204

Cheese and Crackers..206

Chocolate Crush Pie.. 208

Chocolate Mousse... 210

Fruit Crepe...212

Cheesecake... 214

Pink Passion Pie…... 216

Fruit Leather Crepe 218

Coconut Cream Flan Cake with Pineapple Filling..........220

Ice Cream 222

Candy Apples...224

Websites, Videos and other things by Cara and Markus................ 228

Introduction by Markus

I never smoked a cigarette in my life, never drank a drop of alcohol or did any drugs other than what the doctors gave me. I tried to do everything right, yet by the time I was in my late twenties, I was dying. My heart was collapsing, I had glasses thicker than the windshield of my car, my lungs were so filled with fluid I was choking and my digestive system was bleeding. Little did I know it was all because of what I was eating- the standard modern diet. I was lucky. I figured it out. Most don't. The sad thing is that the answer is so simple and easy, anyone can do it. It's really just getting back to how nature designed us, that's it. The healthiest food is all natural things you find in nature- fruit, vegetables, nuts, seeds, greens etc. We are designed to eat ONLY that. The more we eat processed food, the unhealthier we get. Cooking kills the life force in food. We are the only species on the planet that cooks its food, and the only species that consistently gets cancer, diabetes, heart disease and endless other illnesses. The only animals that really get those diseases are those fed by man or eat garbage left over by man.

Another cause of many health problems is food made with wheat flour, which can lead to endless issues including celiac disease, leaky gut syndrome, candida yeast overgrowth, mold in the body, kidney stones, irritable bowel, hypoglycemia, diabetes, and ultimately cancer. It also feeds parasites and makes them grow like crazy. Food made with wheat flour is addictive. It includes bread, pasta, cereal, wraps, burritos, pies, cakes, deserts, cookies, crackers, you name it. When coupled with one of the other most addictive substances on earth - sugar, you have a recipe for disaster. Sure it tastes good- but is it worth losing your health and life?

What if you could still eat foods just like that, but not get sick anymore? In fact, what if you ate similar food but actually got BETTER, healthier, more energy, lost weight, and even started looking up to twenty years younger? Guess what? All you have to do is stop eating man-made crap and start eating the way nature intended- raw, uncooked natural foods using only ingredients found in nature. This does not mean carrot sticks and celery. It does not have to be boring. In fact, if you know how to prepare it, you will be experiencing food like you've never experienced before. It tastes better, looks better and makes you feel better. Eating this kind of food instead of commercial food is comparable to having been a prisoner in an office building for 30 years, then stepping outside into sunshine for the first time, hearing birds sing, feeling a soft breeze on your face, and seeing trees, blue sky and mountains calling your name to adventure and freedom. You are about to enter a whole new way of living, eating and feeling. Your soul will sing knowing you are doing the right thing, and even the way you think will change. People will wonder why you look and act younger and why you seem so peaceful.

Even if you just incorporate one or several of these recipes into your life, you will be one step in the direction of health. We did our best to make the transition as fun, painless and easy as possible by making some of the food look and taste just like the unhealthy versions you grew up with.

Cara and I are very busy just like you and don't have a lot of time or desire to make food, so we figured out ways to make things as fast as possible. There is no oven or stove "cooking" per se, but there is some dehydrating involved, so just whip something up when you go to bed and it will be ready when you wake up… or make something in the morning, and it will be ready for dinner when you finish work. Lunches are usually salads for us, which can be thrown together in a matter of minutes. We also make batches of snack foods like cookies, nut crunches, chips, pop tarts and other fun stuff we can snack on all day. We make enough to carry us through the week, or even take with us when we travel.

Some people may wonder why we have meals imitating the look and taste of meat and animal products when we ourselves are vegan animal lovers. The reason should be obvious and simple. First- most of the world eats meat and is unhealthy, The only way we can get them to start switching over is to give them the same experience they are used to, and at the same time show them that eating healthy is not sacrificing anything in the way of taste, look or smell. We all grew up eating this stuff, got used to it and part of us misses the taste. But we don't want to have to kill animals to get it.
Some may ask if this is a high fat and cholesterol diet. First of all, plants don't have cholesterol. There are good fats and bad fats. The good fats help get rid of the bad fats. Farmers used to feed their cows coconut oil hoping to fatten them up, but instead the cows got lean and healthy. They actually lost weight! Look at Cara and me. We are more fit, thin and healthier than many people half our age. You need healthy fats and oils. Your brain is 80% fat. Without adequate amounts of healthy fats, your body would literally fall apart. Every cell in your body needs healthy oils and fats as much as water. Just make sure you're using the good stuff (coconut, olive, avocado, nuts, seeds etc).

The right way to start your journey to health and vibrant living is three steps:
1. Stop doing what's causing the problems in the first place (unhealthy choices)
2. Do a serious life and body cleanse
3. Rebuild with proper fuel and building materials

At 55, I now look and feel younger than when I was 30. I no longer need glasses or ever get sick. This is all outlined in my core bestselling book "Heal Yourself 101" (now a free download at HealYourselfbook.com)
It introduces you to this lifestyle, lists the main mistakes people make, and walks you through the cleansing and rebuilding process.

Let this uncookbook be your inspiration for a new life!

Introduction by Cara

I have been eating raw foods on and off since I can remember, and I can tell you I've never felt better than when consuming all my food 100% raw.

At age 38, I began a 100% all raw, low calorie diet. What I felt, it just blew my mind away. Aches and pains in my body, from normal wear and tear disappeared. When one would reappear, it would quickly heal itself (faster than in past times I can remember) and the pain would cease. By eating so little, and when I did, only the most healthiest of foods, my body was not spending energy digesting food. It takes a lot of precious energy to digest food. When the body is not busy digesting food, it is in healing and repair mode. That is why my body felt so incredible. Because it had nothing to do but heal whatever ailed me. I find that pretty fascinating. Of course my energy level was through the roof also. Digesting food bogs you down. Makes you tired.

The mental clarity I experienced from this low calorie, raw food diet was impressive as well. Studies are showing that eating fatty, fried and processed foods contributes to diseases in the brain. Makes sense that eating the opposite of that, and very little, would have the opposite effect on the brain. And I'm here to tell you that it does! Scientists have known for a long time now, that spontaneous bouts of hunger cause new neurons to grow in the brain. What you eat, and how much, has a direct correlation on your brain.
When I wasn't eating completely raw, I still made my own food. It consisted of vegetables, barley soups, nature burgers, etc. which I thought were not that bad for me even though they were cooked. I am very in tune with my body. When it loves something I'm doing, I'm rewarded with a radiant glow, lots of energy, ache and pain free, etc… and I can also feel when I'm not eating the best foods for my body. When eating vegan, cooked food, I still felt it causing dis-ease to by body. I felt aches and pains in my joints. My energy levels dropped, my face looked older and a little swollen.

There is just nothing like the feeling you get when eating foods in their natural state. Your main health insurance should be called the "Farmers Market".

For many people, eating healthy can be very complicated and ultimately frustrating. There is so much information out there and so much of it is contradictory. Multi-billion dollar companies employ geniuses to sway us to fork over our hard earned money in exchange for their "food" product that wreaks havoc in the body. But with more and more documentaries being made disclosing the perils of eating animal products, and easy access, via internet into "houses of horrors" that are called factory farms, and with diabetes, cancer and obesity at an all time high, people have no choice but to take heed to what is going on in, and around them.

Yes, things need to change. And I think its very motivating to think just how much positive change can result in the world, as well as the human body, merely by switching over to a mainly plant based diet. When we know better, we typically do better.

You should be spending 95% of your time in the grocery store, in the produce department. Most every other food item there (except for the raw food section), has no beneficial affect on your body.

When my brother, Juliano and I told friends and family we wanted to open an all raw food restaurant people thought we were crazy. Everyone we spoke to about our idea just couldn't grasp the concept. I mean, this was 1994 in Chicago. These people have been eating pizza, pasta and meats their whole lives. When we told them we were going to serve pasta and pizza, thats when things got even more confusing for them. At one point, one old timer wrote us off as losing our minds. In his mind raw, hard pasta and doughy, raw pizza were inedible! My fathers friends and family wouldn't finance us. They actually were worried about us. Our mom financed us, and we opened "Raw" in San Francisco in 1995 and sat, and waited, and waited. Business was severely slow at first because people didn't understand it or know what to make of it. I can't tell you how many times people asked if the pasta was served UN boiled and hard. Or in the "living" sushi recipe, if the fish was still alive. Words like "living" and "raw" had such a different meaning back then than they do today.

But we persevered, coming up with new and exciting dishes everyday for as long as we had to. After 6 months, our restaurant had a review written up in the San Francisco Chronicle by Michael Baur. He is one of the most critical food critics out there. He wrote, in summary, "For a city known for innovative cooking, Raw beats them all!"

That was it. After that article came People, then Vogue, then world wide publications and raw food was now becoming popular! Once word spread that a new restaurant opened, serving delicious, healthy, food prepared in unheard of ways, that make you feel energized afterwards, the flood gates broke. Every publication worldwide wanted to be the first to report about this new, gourmet fair. People began opening their eyes to a new way, a better way of eating and fueling the body. That was over 20 years ago. Back then, there was us and a couple of "hole in the wall" raw cafes sprinkled throughout. Today, there are over 400 raw food restaurants worldwide! That tells me people want better
 for themselves and their loved ones. This book is dedicated to those wanting to do better for them and their world and those they share their world with.

This isn't a diet, it is a way of life!

The Basics

The basics of Raw food is very easy. Never heat anything above 118 F (45) or else the life-force in the food will be killed, especially the enzymes. How would you like to be boiled or baked? You would die. Same with the food you eat. Food with life gives you life. In nature, things dehydrate on hot days. Fruit may shrivel up and dry but it's still nutritious. If you plant it in the ground, it still retains the power to grow another plant. This is the basis of dehydrating. Sure it takes longer, but you'll live longer. Just because something takes 10 hours to dehydrate, you should not say "it took me 10 hours to make this!". No it didn't. It took you maybe 10 minutes to prepare it, you stuck it in the dehydrator and went to work. When you came home, it was ready. Or you went to sleep and when you woke up, it was ready. Do you see how this works? It's working hard while you are away. You personally don't have to do very much at all.

But not everything has to be dehydrated. In fact, you can live without one if you want. It's just nice to have warm stuff right out of the machine, and, as you'll see in the book, this process allows you to make some amazing things, that look and taste better than their dead-food counterparts. You can taste the life still in this food!

The most used piece of equipment is the Vitamix. We use it for almost everything. It's a very powerful blender and it's one of the best investments you can make for your health and busy lifestyle. Always keep the top on when using it. Get to know how to use the plunger (tamper)- it reaches down to just above the spinning blades and helps push the food into the blades. One of the most important things to know about using it is to scrape downwards in each corner as the unit is on. The thicker the stuff you are mixing, the harder and faster you need to thrust the plunger- just like a toilet plunger, you want to create a "force field" at the end of the plunger that rams the stubborn food down into the vortex, with fast hard jabbing motions down each corner.

When dehydrating, you will need the standard mesh screens, but also a bunch of Teflex sheets. These are slippery sheets that can hold runny stuff without leaking, so watery things can dry into patties. Remember when using the Teflex sheets, that no air gets to the underside, so the top gets hard and crusty, but the bottom is stiff gooey, so after a few hours, you need to flip the item so the underside can dry also. This is demonstrated on page 16.

Overall, this stuff is fast and easy once you get the hang of it. We are busy just like you and don't have a lot of time or desire to make food, so we figured out ways to make things as fast as possible. With a little understanding of how to keep life-force intact in your food, this can become a lot of fun. Let this book be an inspiration to jump start your own creativity!

We will be posting regular videos, recipes and articles on our newsletter- MarkusNews.com, so sign up, it's free and will give you lots of eye-opening ways to supercharge your life to a new way of living!

THINGS TO ALWAYS HAVE AVAILABLE

VITAMIX BLENDER
Blendtec is also powerful
The Markus blender should be out soon.
Check MarkusNews.com

SOFT COCONUT MEAT
The meat from young Thai coconuts eels just like meat. Scoop your own coconuts or buy ready from health store freezer section, or have it shipped to you from online.

DEHYDRATOR
Many to choose from. Excalibur is a good company. Be sure to get both screen mesh and Teflex sheets (about 6-9 each)

CASHEWS
Not totally raw (steam extracted) but still healthy and indispensable for making almost any kind of recipe.

COFFEE GRINDER
Used to grind nuts, cacao nibs etc into powder

ALMONDS
Get organic. Most commercial almonds aren't raw anymore, but still better than not having them.

OFFSET SPATULA
Helps get things out of blender and smear paste evenly flat on dehydrator sheets. Also helps lift flat cakes etc.

FROZEN BANANAS
Keep a bunch in zip lock bag in freezer for smoothies etc.

CELTIC Sea salt
This is by far the best salt from our experience, much better than Himalayan etc.
The coarse grind is more flavorful.

APPLE CIDER VINEGAR
Can't live without this stuff! (never use white vinegar) ACV is super healing to the body, helps digestion and nutrients absorb better. It's like good tasting medicine!

NUT MILK/CREME
Make your own and have it ready for everything.
See recipe page 18

NUTRITIONAL YEAST
Great for adding cheesy flavor to things. Great source of vitamins. This is a healthy yeast and does not feed Candida.

COCONUT OIL
A healthy oil that helps get rid of bad fats in your body. Actually helps you lose weight. Great sweet taste.

DATES
A great sweetener, and very nutritious. One single date can be considered a meal

OLIVE OIL
Extra Virgin Cold Pressed

MARKUSSWEET
The best all natural sugar subsitute you can get.
Zero calories! Zero Glycemic. Zero Insulin, not fattening
Great for diabetics.
Tastes & used just like sugar.

SEA MOSS
A yellowish clear seaweed that gels & thickens things. Great for cheesecakes, cheeses, etc. Don't use powder or flakes, they don't work. Get it at MarkusProducts.com

MAPLE SYRUP
Nothing beats the taste.
A little fattening but much better for you than Agave, honey, coconut sugar. Lots of minerals and a strong antioxidant.

DRIED MULBERRIES
We get them at Whole Foods but you can order them online. Great for adding to fruit salads and adding crunch to fruit smoothies and deserts. Dehydrate more for crunch.

NAMA SHOYU
Unpasteurized soy sauce. You can get it online. If you can't get it, use low sodium Tamari sauce

Flipping Things over while Drying

Teflex sheets are used for watery, runny things that drip. But air can't get to the underside of food, so it needs to be flipped once the upper side gets hard enough. This is how to do it. It's fast and easy. It's best to flip it things onto a screen mesh once one side has a solid enough surface, so air can get through the mesh and als dry from underneath.

When food develops crust on top, it's ready to flip

Place mesh screen on top along with second tray

Hold the two trays together like a sandwich and flip over

Delicately peel off the Teflex sheet

Place back in dehydrator on screen mesh this time

Basic Elements

Cashew Vanilla Silk Milk

1 1/2 cups cashews, soaked 1 hour
3/4 to 1 cup water
1/4 teaspoon vanilla
2 tablespoons maple syrup

Place cashews, sweetener & vanilla in blender. Pour 1/2 cup of the water in blender and blend for 30 seconds until thick, smooth cream. You want to add just enough water so that the cashews will blend together. Too much water during this first step will leave milk grainy, not silky smooth. Add rest of water or until desired consistency.
Refrigerate in glass jars. Lasts 3 - 5 days.

Savory Cream

Makes about 2 cups
1 1/2 cups un-soaked cashews
1 1/4 cups water
pinch salt

Put cashews in blender with 1/2 cup of water and blend. After a few seconds slowly add more water until the nuts are almost completely broken up then add rest of water and blend till smooth.

Sweet Cream

1 1/2 cups cashews (unsoaked)
2 tablespoons maple syrup or MarkusSweet
1 tablespoon vanilla
1 cup water

Place nuts, sweetener and 1/4 cup of the water in blender. Blend and slowly add rest of water until smooth. Cream stiffens as it chills.

Interesting fact: Did you know Maple Syrup has more nutrients than honey, is anti-inflammatory and a super powerful antioxidant? It doesn't spike sugar in your body like other sweeteners.

Sea moss

A natural Gel and thickener

Sea moss is a seaweed full of minerals and nutrients, that also happens to be a great way to add gel consistency to foods. We use it to make cheese, desserts, cakes, flan, meat substitutes and all kinds of fun things. Do not use Sea moss powder or flakes- those have had all the gel and nutrients cooked out of them. In it's natural form, it comes in bags, preserved in salt and needs to be washed and soaked multiple times to get rid of the smell, sand and ocean grit. This stuff not only thickens your hair, it's "nature's collagen" and helps plump up your skin and hair. Forget plastic surgery- use Sea moss! You can get it at MarkusSeaMoss.com

Sea Moss Gel

Yields 3 cups
2 cups packed soaked sea moss
1/4 to 1/2 cups water

Rinse Sea moss in a large colander picking out any debris. Rinse extremely well under kitchen faucet or take outside and spray with garden hose while in colander. Add to large glass bowl and cover with water. Soak for 2 hours. Drain and rinse and add to blender with water and blend on low for at least 90 seconds. Add more water if Sea moss seems dry, isn't turning over or is not at a creamy consistency yet. Refrigerate in glass jars. Lasts 2 weeks.

We sell it in 1 lb bags at MarkusProducts.com. It expands to 4 times its size when wet and lasts for weeks in the refrigerator prepared (lasts a year dry in bag)

Learn more about it and watch me prepare some in a video at MarkusSeaMoss.com

Sea Moss

Almond Cheese

Can be cut like Mozzarella or crumbled like Feta

2 cups organic almonds, soaked for an hour
1 cup sea moss gel
1 cup water
1/2 cup green onion, finely sliced
1 tablespoon truffle or olive oil
1 teaspoon fresh dill, minced (optional)
1 teaspoon salt
1 tablespoon nutritional yeast (optional)
1/4 teaspoon black pepper

Blanch almonds by pinching them out at the wider bottom. They will easily pop out of their skin after an hour. Place almonds and Sea moss in blender with 3/4 cup of water and turn on high. Use blender tamper to help blend almonds. Only add just enough water to help turn over ingredients. Stir in the remaining ingredients, mold and chill in fridge. Will last for 5 days in fridge.

Can also be made with (unsoaked) cashews instead of almonds.

For Ricotta cheese, add 2 tablespoons water to make it creamier and fluffier

See video at RawAlmondCheese.com

Garlic Naan
Makes 2 slices

Blend:
2 cups coconut meat
1 cup white onion, shredded then all mositure pressed out using cheesecloth or strainer

<u>Sprinkle on top:</u>
1/4 cup onion pieces
2 garlic cloves, minced
1 tablespoon olive oil
1/4 teaspoon thyme
1/2 teaspoon curly parsley, minced
pinch salt

Blend coconut meat and onion till smooth. Pour half of mixture onto Teflex sheet and spread evenly using an offset spatula or gently drop tray onto counter a couple times as this evens out the mixture as well.
Dehydrate at 120 for a few hours before checking if naan bread easily tears away from sheet without sticking to it. If so, it's time to flip onto a mesh sheet so drying time is achieved more evenly. Naan is ready when completely dry, anywhere from 6 to 12 hours depending on climate and dehydrator.

See video at GarlicNaan.com

Deli

Lunch Meat Slices
2/3 cup sea moss
1 cup coconut meat
1 teaspoon chipotle powder
1/4 cup orange bell pepper
3 tablespoons Nama Shoyu
2 tablespoons chopped Sun dried tomatoes

Blend ingredients in blender, pour on dehydrator sheets into round shapes and spread flat and evenly with offset spatula. Dehydrate 2 hours at 118F (45) until crust forms, then flip over onto screen sheet, continue dehydrating until ready.

Cheese Slices
1 cup fresh washed and soaked Sea Moss
1/2 cup coconut meat
1/4 cup cashews or almonds
3 tablespoons apple cider vinegar
2 tablespoons nutritional yeast
1/2 teaspoon paprika
1/4 teaspoon sea salt
minced red and green spicy peppers (add after blending)

Add 1/2 cup Agar flakes (or 1/4 cup agar powder) to 1 cup water. Bring to boil, (it's ok, its only the thickener) then reduce heat and simmer at lowest heat for 10 minutes, stirring constantly. (After simmering 10 minutes, it probably will be reduced down to 1/2 cup) Add with other ingredients into blender and blend really well until warm and creamy smooth (no lumps). Mix in minced spicy red and green pepper pieces (like Serrano & Santa Fe peppers) and pour onto smoothTeflex sheet and smear evenly to cheese-slice thickness with offset spatula. Cover with another Teflex sheet (to give it smooth surface) and let sit at room temp for several hours as it gels and hardens. Peel off sheets and cut into single serve squares.

Chips page 96

See videos at **VeganDeliMeat.com** and **HealthyCheese.com**

Burger Patty
Makes 2 patties

1 cup sunflower seeds, soaked for an hour and drained
1 cup walnuts, soaked for an hour and drained
1 cup almonds, soaked for an hour and drained
2-3 medium size carrots
quarter piece of a red beet (for coloring)

1 tablespoon Braggs aminos
1-2 tablespoons olive oil
1/2 cup minced parsley
salt and pepper to taste

Put first 4 ingredients through Champion or twin gear juicer or put in food processor till well ground. Put in bowl and stir in remaining ingredients except for paprika and chipotle powder. Shape like a patty and sprinkle the paprika and chipotle powder all over the top. Drizzle a little more olive oil over patty and dehydrate on mesh sheet at 118F (45c) for 3 hours.

Mustard, Mayonaise, Relish, Ketchup
Lasts several weeks in Refrigerator

Mustard

1/4 cup water
1/4 cup apple cider vinegar
1/4 cup mustard seed powder
1/2 avocado
3 tablespoons MarkusSweet
2 tablespoons olive oil
1 teaspoon paprika
1/2 teaspoon turmeric
1/2 teaspoon Celtic sea salt

For Dijon, blend until smooth
For stone ground, don't blend totally smooth,
mix in 1 tablespoon whole mustard seed after
blending

Relish

1 cucumber (2.5 cups)
1/3 cup apple cider vinegar
3/4 teaspoon Celtic sea salt
1 tablespoon MarkusSweet

Chop in food processor
Drain liquid through strainer
Add 1-2 tablespoon apple cider vinegar

Mayonaise

1- 1.5 cup coconut meat
1/2 cup apple cider vinegar
6 tablespoons olive oil
1 tablespoon pine nuts
1 teaspoon Celtic sea salt
1 tablespoon water

Blend until super smooth

Ketchup

3/4 cup fresh tomatoes
1/2 cup sun dried tomatoes
3 teaspoons apple cider vinegar
1 teaspoon olive oil
1 date or1 tablespoon MarkusSweet
1/2 teaspoon onion powder
1/2 teaspoon paprika
1/4 teaspoon Celtic sea salt
pinch cayenne

Blend until smooth

Thousand Island Dressing is on page 144

See videos for each at KetchupMustard.com

Creamy Mashed Potatoes, Veggies & Onion Rings

Serves 3
Mashed Potatoes
1 cup zucchini, peeled and chopped
1 cup & 2 tablespoons of cashews, soaked for 40 minutes
1 cup chopped cauliflower
1/2 garlic clove
2 tablespoons olive oil
1 tablespoon nutritional yeast
salt & pepper
1/2 teaspoon finely chopped fresh thyme
1/4 teaspoon finely chopped fresh rosemary

Add first 4 ingredients in order to blender. No water is necessary as the zucchini are 96% water and will liquify as soon as the blades touch them. Turn on blender and use tamper to push ingredients down to the blade. Let run for 10 seconds then serve. Add olive oil, nutritional yeast and salt to small bowl and whisk. Pour over potatoes and sprinkle the minced herbs and salt & pepper to taste.

Onion Rings
1 onion, sliced into 1/4 inch thick slices
2 cups ground up flax cracker(page 36) has richer taste than just plain ground flax
1/2 teaspoon thyme
1/4 teaspoon salt
poultry seasoning
1/2 cup savory cream (page 18)
1 tablespoon olive oil

Add flax powder,spices and seasoning to a bowl. Pour the cream into a different bowl. Put onions in cream and jiggle to evenly coat. Lift and put in flax crumb bowl and coat well. Lay out on dehydrator sheet & repeat till all onions are coated. Drizzle oil all over onions and dehydrate for 8 hours.

Vegetable prepartion on page 168   A simpler version of onion rings is on page 92

Bacon/Meat/Jerky

1 cup coconut meat
1 tablespoon Nama Shoyu
1/2 teaspoon paprika
1/2 teaspoon chipotle powder

Cut coconut meat into strips and place on dehydrator sheet. Rub remaining ingredients all over coconut and dehydrate for at least 3 hours. For Jerky, dehydrate overnight.

See video at VeganBacon.com

Fruit Cracker

Makes 1 tray
2 cups golden flax
2 cups orange juice
2 tablespoons maple syrup
1 cup frozen blueberries or raspberries, thawed
1/2 cup frozen cranberries, thawed
1/2 cup fresh pineapple, cut into thin slices

Soak flax seeds in orange juice for an hour or until seeds soften. If mixture becomes too dry add some orange juice and stir well. Add enough orange juice so that mixture is like oatmeal consistency. Stir in remaining ingredients and pour out onto dehydrator sheet. Spread evenly 1/4 inch thick and dehydrate at 118F (45c) for 2 hours. Flip onto mesh, add chocolate drizzle and dehydrate till crispy.

Chocolate Syrup
Makes 1 cup

1 cup cacao powder
1/2 cup plus 1 tablespoon maple syrup
1/2 cup plus 2 tablespoons cashew milk (page 18)
splash vanilla
tiny pinch salt
Blend all ingredients on high. Put in jar & refrigerate. Lasts 2 days.

Drinks

Green Smoothie

This is the easiest start of the raw food journey and should be a regular way to start your day. If you do nothing else, at least do green smoothies. It's the best, fastest way to get super healing nutrition into your body. The basic rule is half greens, half fruit, 2 cups liquid and some herbal plant powders like Wild Force Greens and Protein (because grocery produce doesn't usually have all the nutrients you need). The variations are endless. Use whatever is in season or available. Markus often goes in the front yard and uses wild weeds as greens.
Frozen bananas help thicken the drink. Add 1-2 tablespoon Udo's 369 oil for Essential Omega oils

Green Suggestions: kale, celery, parsley, dandelion, watercress, red leaf lettuce, anything green

Fruit suggestions: Any frozen fruit, strawberries, blueberries, pineapple, papaya, cranberries etc

Liquid suggestions: plain water, coconut water, orange juice. (Don't use apple juice-too much sugar)

Herbal Supplement Suggestions: 2 tablespoons each of Markus Wild Force Greens and Super Protein

Strawberry Smoothie
Serves 2

2 cups frozen strawberries
2 tablespoons maple syrup
2 ice cubes
1 cup nut milk (page 18)
1 cup sweet cream (page 18)

Put everything but sweet cream in blender and blend just until contents turn over and ingredients are all blended. Fill only 1/4 of the glass w smoothie then add a layer of sweet cream. Twirl glass while spooning sweet cream in to get it all around glass. Sprinkle some candied travel nuts (page 88), then more smoothie & repeat till glass is full.

Cactus Aloe Smoothie

4 cups prickly pear (Nopales) cactus (handle with tongs)
1 cup aloe vera, somewhat skinned
2 cups orange juice

Blend at high speed until total liquid

Strain through nut milk bag

Drink.

See video at CactusAloe.com

Raspberry Mint Lime Cocktail

Serves 2

1/2 cup frozen raspberries, half way thawed
1/2 cup lime juice
1/3 cup maple syrup
1 cup loosely packed mint
3 1/2 cups good water

Add all ingredients to blender and blend on high for 10 seconds.

Grapefruit Garlic Ginger Daydream
Serves 2

1 1/2 cups fresh squeezed juice from cold grapefruits.
1 teaspoon minced fresh ginger
1 garlic clove
1 tablespoon olive oil (not a typo, it's good for the body and dee-licious in this drink!)
Put all ingredients in blender and blend on high for 5 seconds. Enjoy immediately!

SERVING SUGGESTION: Add 1 1/2 tablespoons of sweet cashew milk (page 18) to drink after poured into glasses. Garnish w/ a thin grapefruit slice that's been brushed w/ coconut oil, sprinkled with poppy seeds and dehydrated.

Veggie Juice

Juice fresh seasonal juices like:

Kale
Spinach
Celery
Parsley
Dandelion
Carrots
Carrot Greens
Beets
Beet Greens
Green Apples
Lemon

Add some Ginger

Must drink right away because juices oxidize quickly
and lose their nutrient value within 30 minutes.
(Blender drinks can last until tomorrow)

Gourmet Chocolate milk

12 cacao beans
1 coconut- meat and coconut water
7 cashews
1 big tablespoon coconut oil
3 teaspoons maple syrup
1/2 teaspoon cinnamon
pinch of sea salt

Blend and Enjoy

Green Dream Juice
2 Servings

1 green apple
3 celery stalks
half of a cucumber
1 garlic clove
1 one inch piece of ginger
1 lemon (whole)

Wash and cut up all ingredients to fit into juicer chute. Push through juicer and drink immediately. The moment fresh squeezed green juice is exposed to air it's live enzymes begin degrading, diminishing nutritional content.

Lemongrass Ginger Chuenchai
2 Servings

1 cup fresh squeezed orange juice
1/2 cup fresh squeezed lime
1 frozen banana
1 tablespoons finely minced lemongrass
3/4 teaspoon Nama Shoyu (organic, raw soy sauce)

Add all ingredients to blender and blend for 10 seconds. Strain through fine mesh. Serve immediately

Pumpkin or Strawberry Parfait
Serves 2

1 1/2 cups pumpkin, peeled & chopped small (or 4 large strawberries cut up)
1/2 cup coconut cream
1/2 cup thicker cashew cream
1 1/2 tablespoons maple syrup
1 cap full vanilla
1/4 teaspoon nutmeg
1/3 teaspoon cinnamon
Add all ingredients to blender and blend
on high pushing ingredients down with tamper
until creamy smooth.

Toppings
whipped cashew cream (page 18)
candied almonds (page 88)
fresh fruit
mint leaf

Pour a short layer of the pumpkin into center of glass. Layer a swirl of cashew cream around the glass followed by a sprinkle of candied nuts. Repeat process till glass is full.

For Strawberry Parfait drop a few strawberry slices into a glass. Layer a swirl of cashew cream on top of berries twisting glass as you spread. Add a sprinkle of candied nuts and repeat till at top of glass. Garnish w/ mint leaf.

Chocolate Smoothie
Serves 2

2/3 cup chocolate syrup (page 35)
3/4 cup cashew milk (page 18)
1/4 ripe avacado
3 tablespoons maple syrup
12 ice cubes

Put everything in blender and use tamper to help turn things over. Blend just until contents turn over and ingredients are blended. Fill only 1/4 of the glass, then add a layer of whip cream. Twirl glass while spooning whip cream in to get it all around glass. Sprinkle some candied travel nuts next (page 88) then more smoothie & repeat till glass is full.

TOPPING SUGGESTION: Chocolate syrup (see page 36), raspberry syrup (bag of frozen raspberries thawed and blended), pomegranate seeds, cacao nibs, fresh fruit, mint leaf, dried mulberries-dehydrated for a few hours then minced.

Pina Colada

2 servings

For the best tasting pinia colada, this recipe will have you easily making your own coconut cream!

Coconut Cream
1 1/2 heaping cups unsweetened, dried coconut
1 1/3 cup warm good water
Blend all ingredients on high for 1 minute. Pour mixture into a nut milk bag (or through fine strainer) and squeeze liquid out into container. Pour into a glass and refrigerate a few hours up to 24 hours. Cream will have risen to top when ready.

Place the following in blender:
1 cup frozen, pineapple chunks
3/4 cup pineapple juice
1 tablespoon Markus sugar or sweetener of choice
coconut cream (in glass in frigerator)
Blend on high speed until smooth, 10 to 20 seconds. Pour in glass and garnish with a pineapple wedge and piece of strawberry. Sprinkle cacau nibs on for added texture!

For the freshest pineapple juice, peel a pineapple, core it (eat core, super healthy!), chop into chunks and toss in blender. Pulse a few times till chunks are shredded. Pour contents into a nut milk bag and squeeze juice out into container.

See video at HealthyPinaColada.com

Edible Flower pictured: Hibiscus

Soups

Bangkok Thai Soup
Yields approximately 2 cups

1 1/2 cups soaked cashews
1 cup water
3 tablespoons chopped ginger
1 tablespoon chopped garlic
2 tablespoons finely chopped lemongrass
(2 tablespoons finely chopped lime leaf, kifer lime or any leaf from a citrus tree if available)
1 tablespoon Braggs liquid amino's
2 tablespoons fresh lime juice

Add all ingredients to blender except water, Braggs and lime juice. Start by adding 1/2 cup of the water to blender and turn on high. Allow nuts to break up and blend a few seconds than slowly drizzle the rest of the water into blender while blender is on. Turn on low and add the Braggs and lime juice. Soup will thicken in fridge. Add a little water to soup to thin after chilling.

SERVING SUGGESTION: Serve over finely shredded purple cabbage, cherry tomatoes cut in half, chives, mushrooms that have marinated a while in oil and Nama Shoyu. Add jalapeño or red pepper flakes for a kick.

unChicken Noodle Soup
Serves 2

(dehydrator)
2 oyster mushrooms
2 celery ribs, sliced in 1/4 inch pieces
1 carrot, cut in 1/4 inch pieces
1 small onion, in 1/4 inch wedges
1 tablespoon olive oil
Salt & pepper to taste

(blender)
1 cup water
1/2 teaspoon fresh thyme
1/2 teaspoon onion powder
1 teaspoon oil
1/2 teaspoon Nama Shoyu (organic, raw soy sauce)
1/2 clove garlic

1/2 cup pasta noodles (page 154)

Shred oyster mushrooms a bit by pulling them apart with your fingers. Add to bowl with next 4 ingredients. Put onto dehydrator sheet and sprinkle with salt & pepper. Dehydrate for 5 hours or until soft. Check regularly to ensure veggies aren't drying out. Drizzle more oil if so. Divide veggies and pasta evenly in 2 bowls and blend next 5 ingredients. Pour over veggies.

SERVING SUGGESTION: Top with fresh minced parsley

Corn Chowder
2 servings

1 one pound bag organic frozen corn, thawed
1 1/2 cups minced white onion
1 teaspoon minced garlic
1 tablespoon thyme
3 tablespoons olive oil
4 tablespoons savory cashew cream (page 18)
salt and pepper to taste

Place corn, onion, olive, garlic and oil in a bowl and toss well to coat. Lay out evenly on dehydrator sheet. Season with thyme, salt and pepper. Dehydrate for 3 to 3 1/2 hours at 118.

Take corn mixture and add to high speed blender or food processor with savory, cashew cream and pulse blend a few times. We don't want to cream the ingredients, just pulse chop a few times. Pour into serving bowls and add optional garnishes above.

Optional garnishes
Thinly sliced green onion, fennel, red pepper flakes, fresh garlic, truffle or olive oil, "bacon bits (page 34)

Salads

Markus Basic Kale Salad

Salad
1 head kale
1 thick slice fresh pineapple, cubed
1 avocado, cubed
1/2 red onion, cubed
3 dates, pitted and cubed

Dressing
2 tablespoons olive oil
2 tablespoons toasted sesame oil
3 tablespoons apple cider vinegar
1/2 teaspoon coarse grind Celtic sea salt
pinch black pepper

Top with pine nuts and pumpkin seeds

Cheese, Date Pineapple Salad
Serves 2

1 cups cubed cheese (page 22)
6 dates, cut in half then half again
2 cups kale, torn into bite size pieces
2 cups pineapple, cubed
1 cup spiced, candied cashews
2 green scallions, chopped

Dressing (whisk in bowl till creamy)
3 tablespoons olive oil
3 tablespoons balsamic vinegar
2 tablespoons apple cider vinegar
2 tablespoons nutritional yeast
salt & pepper to taste

Ricotta Cheese- Makes about 2 cups

2 cups organic almonds
1 cup Sea moss
1 cup (add 2 tablespoons extra water for ricotta) good water

Soak almonds for 45 minutes in good water. Skin almonds by pinching at the fatter tip. Add Sea moss and 1/2 cup of the water to blender. Blend on high till nuts are creamed. Add a little drizzle if blender is having trouble turning over. Once creamed add remaining water and blend well. Let firm in fridge a few hours.

For **Feta cheese**, just add 2 tablespoons less water to make it more crumbly

Greek Salad
Serves 1

3 leaves of romaine torn into 1 inch pieces
1/2 tomato, quartered
5 cucumber slices
2 slices purple onion
5 mint leaves
1 teaspoon parsley, minced
4 kalamata olives
1 1/2 tablespoons feta cheese (page 74), crumbled
1/2 garlic clove, minced
1/2 teaspoon minced fresh oregano

Add first 7 salad ingredients to bowl. Pour dressing over and top w/ cheese, garlic, oregano, salt & pepper.

Dressing
1 1/2 tablespoons apple cider or red wine vinegar
3/4 teaspoon fresh lemon juice
3 tablespoons olive oil

Edible Flower pictured: Pansy

Green Crunch Salad
Serves 1

1 large kale leaf, rolled up and sliced
1/2 tomato, quartered
few slices purple onion
1/4 avocado, cut in desired shape
1/3 cup crumbled kale chips (page 92)

Mix into bowl (or collard green leaf as pictured). Add dressing of choice followed by sprinkling the spirulina evenly on top. Finish w/ salt & pepper.

Basic Dressing
2 teaspoons olive oil
1 teaspoon lemon juice
1/2 tablespoon apple cider vinegar
1/2 tablespoon spirulina powder
Salt & pepper to taste

Tahini Dressing
1 tablespoon tahini
1 teaspoon mellow white or yellow miso
1 teaspoon lemon juice
1 teaspoon apple cider vinegar
1 teaspoon good water
1 tablespoon olive oil
Place all ingredients except for oil in a deep bowl. Whisk till smooth then while continuing whisking, drizzle the olive oil into the dressing.

Asian Salad
Serves 1

Salad
1/2 cup thinly shredded purple cabbage
1/2 cup pasta
8 mint leaves
quarter red pepper, sliced
1 tablespoon cilantro
2 tablespoon chopped pineapple
1 green onion, thinly sliced
1/2 tablespoon ginger
1/2 tablespoon garlic

Dressing
1 tablespoon cashew butter
1 teaspoon light or yellow miso
1/2 teaspoon Nama Shoyu
1/2 tablespoon organic rice wine vinegar
1/2 tablespoon maple syrup
1 tablespoon fresh lime juice
1 tablespoon good water
1 tablespoon toasted or regular sesame seed oil

Whisk dressing ingredients together till creamy smooth and pour over salad.

Seaweed Salad
Serves 2

Salad:
1 cup 5 colored seaweed (or favorite sea veggies)
1/2 cup zuchini pasta (like from page 154)
1 green onion, 1/4 inch slices
1/4 cup cilantro, chopped
1 tablespoon curly parsley, finely minced
10 mint leaves, torn
1/2 avocado, cubed
1/2 cup cherry tomatos, halved
1 tablespoon ginger, minced
1/2 tablespoon garlic, minced
1 1/2 tablespoons lime juice
1 1/2 tablespoons olive oil
2 nori sheets (sushi wrappers)

Top with:
1 tablespoons sesame seeds
1/2 teaspoon sesame oil
2 nori sheets (optional)

Add salad ingredients to large bowl. Crumble one of the nori sheets into small pieces onto salad. Gently stir until all ingredients are combined well. Add 3 drops sesame oil and sprinkle sesame seeds.

Tabouli Salad

Serves 2

1/2 cup soaked barley (soak for 5 hours)
1 cup soaked and sprouted quinoa
1 tomato, finely chopped
3/4 cup chopped cucumber
1/4 cup red pepper, chopped
1 scallion, chopped
1 cup parsley, finely minced
1/2 cup mint, roughly chopped
1/2 cup cilantro, chopped
1/3 cup lime juice
1/3 cup olive oil

Mix all ingredients up in a bowl.
SERVING SUGGESTION: Top w/ avocado cubes, truffle or olive oil, minced garlic.

See video at RawTabouli.com

Snacks

Almond Nut Crunch
Makes 3/4 tray

2 cups almonds (preferably soaked and dehydrated till real crunchy)
1/2 brazil nuts, thinly sliced
4 tablespoons maple syrup
2 tablespoons golden or other raisin
2 tablespoon currents
2 tablespoon dried cranberry
1/2 teaspoon cinnamon (optional)

Put almonds in processor and pulse a few times until pieces are size in picture. Put in large bowl with remaining ingredients and stir well to combine. Lay out on dehydrator mesh sheet and dehydrate for 3 hours to overnight at 118 degrees F (45c).

This recipe was made famous by the "Cara Stewardess" video which you can watch online at StewardessVideo.com.

Freezer Chocolate

This chocolate gets hard within 30 minutes of being out in the freezer. It can be kept in the freezer indefinitely, but needs to be eaten right away when taken out because coconut oils melts at room temperature. This means it remains liquid inside the body also, unlike hydrogenated fats and oils in commercial chocolate. Pure raw coconut oil is really good for you.

1 cup cacao powder (sifted to remove lumps)
1/4 cup carob powder (sifted to remove lumps)
1/4 to 1/2 cup cashew butter
1/4 cup maple syrup
1/2 cup coconut oil (warmed to clear liquid at room temp)
1 teaspoon vanilla

Mix in bowl, pour in mold or dip things in it and put in freezer. Ready in 1 hour. Eat right away.

Marzipan

1 1/2 cups almond meal
1/4 cup maple syrup

Mix well and knead into dough. You can eat immediately or dip in chocolate that hardens. Stores in refrigerator for long time.

Almond meal is simply almonds ground into fine powder in coffee grinder. For clean colored marzipan, use skinned or blanched almonds

See video at FreezerChocolate.com

Dried Tomatoes, Cheese & Tiny Onion Rings

Cheese   (note: you can mix this cheese with kale and dehydrate to make kale chips)
1 cup cashews
1 red bell pepper
1/2 cup nutritional yeast
1/4 cup pine nuts
3 cloves garlic
1/2 cup water
1/4 cup apple cider vinegar
pinch sea salt

Onion Rings
Slice red onion, take small rings and soak in Nama Shoyu for 30 minutes (soy sauce)

Grind some golden flax seeds in coffee grinder and dip soaked onion rings in the powder to coat them.

Place sliced tomatoes on dehydrator sheet, top with cheese and onion rings on top of that.

Dehydrate 8-10 hrs

Real Potato Chips

Slice potatoes, yams or sweet potatoes on mandolin.
Soak a few hours in water, then drain to get rid of some of the starch.
Soak in mixture of apple cider vinegar and sea salt overnight.
Olive oil is optional.

Dehydrate

Voila.

See video at SimplePotatoChips.com

Chips for Dips

Sweet Chips

1 cup yellow raisins
1 cup nutritional yeast
1 cup ground golden flax
2/3 cup water
1 /3 cup apple cider vinegar
1 teaspoon celtic sea salt
1 tablespoon coconut oil
5 tablespoons maple syrup

Ritz crackers that look like potato chips

2 cups water
1 cup ground white chia seeds
1 cup nutritional yeast
2 tablespoon apple cider vinegar
1/2 teaspoon sea salt
3 teaspoon paprika
1 yellow bell pepper
1 orange bell pepper
(optional) 3 teaspoons turmeric to make more yellow

Make little mounds on dehydrator sheets. After 4-5 hours, flip over onto screen mesh and dehydrate another 4-5 hours or overnight

Chocolate Almond Flax Cookies
Makes a dozen medium cookies

1 cup dry golden flax
1 1/2 cups fresh squeezed orange juice
3 tablespoons maple syrup
1 tablespoon grated orange rind
1/2 cup sliced blanched almonds
2 tablespoons dried currants
2 tablespoons raisins
2 tablespoons frozen rasperries, thawed

Put first 3 ingredients in a large bowl, stir and let soak for 2 1/2 hours. Stir in remaining ingredients, pour onto dehydrator sheet. Spread evenly 1/4 inch thick across sheet. Dehydrate for 2 hours at 118F (45c) then flip onto mesh sheet and continue dehydrating for another hour. Flip and use circle cookie cutter to create cookie shapes. Drizzle chocolate syrup over each cookie then continue to dehydrate another 2 hours or until crisp.

Chocolate Syrup

1 cup cacao powder
1/2 cup plus 1 tablespoon maple syrup
1/2 cup plus 2 tablespoons cashew milk (page 18)
splash vanilla
tiny pinch salt
Put all ingredients in blender and blend on high. Put in jar & refrigerate. Lasts 2 days.

Orange Slices w Protein Powder

A GREAT source of bioflavonoids and fiber, these treats help clean the liver and feed probiotics. They might look strange but they are amazing!

4 naval oranges
3 tablespoons coconut oil
3 tablespoons Markus Wild Force protein powder

Wash and slice oranges quarter inch thick on mandolin. Melt coconut oil by putting sealed bottle in a bowl of hot water for a few minutes. Lay out orange slices in one layer and brush top sides with coconut oil. Sprinkle a little of the Markus Wild Force protein powder (has a great taste with this) on top of of orange slices and spread evenly. Dehydrate for at least 8 hours at 118 degrees F (45).

SERVING SUGGESTION: Sprinkle Green formula and vitamin C powder on some.

Watch this recipe being made at SpyGirlRecipe.com- the hottest recipe video ever!

Chocolate Dipped Almond Cookies

Yields 6 small cookies
2 cups of rolled oats
1 1/2 tablespoon cashew butter
3 tablespoons maple syrup or other sweetener
2 cups apple, grated on the large tooth, peel on (juice included)
3/4 cup chocolate syrup
1/4 cup chopped almonds
splash vanilla

Put rolled oats, **one cup at a time** into a dry blender and turn on high till oats have turned to powder. Pour out into bowl and repeat with second cup of rolled oats. Pour into same bowl and set aside.
 In clean large bowl add the cashew butter and syrup and whisk until satiny smooth and well blended.
Add oat powder and salt and stir, mash and smear, squeeze… until blended as well as possible. Will be super dry at this point. Add grated apple with it's juice to bowl and combine very well. Add almonds
Shape into small cookies. Dip or spread chocolate syrup over half of cookie and dehydrate till desired consistency which is anywhere from 1 minute to a few hours.

SERVING SUGGESTION: For chocolate chip cookies add 1/2 teaspoon more syrup & 1/3 cup cacao nibs.

Apple RAVIOLI

Wrapper:
3 apples, Fuji or Golden Delicious
4 tablespoons coconut ol, melted
2 teaspoons cinnamon
4 tablespoons maple syrup
Peel apples and slice quarter inch thick on mandolin. Cover a glass square container with a single layer of the apple slices. Drizzle with coconut oil and maple syrup and cinnamon and cover with another layer and repeat till all apple slices are well coated with the oil. Remove trays from dehydrator and place glass bowl on the bottom of the dehydrator and turn on high for 20 minutes (according to Excalibur, when sitting foods in a bowl in the dehydrator with liquids it is recommended to turn your dial all the way on high) or until apple slices have softened. Remove and lay apple slices out in single layer on dehydrator sheet.

Filling:
1 cup pecans
1 tablespoon maple syrup
1/2 teaspoon vanilla
3/4 cup good water
Place all ingredients in blender and blend on high till very smooth.

Put a dollop of filling in center of apple slice. Cover with another apple slice and gently press around the edges to seal. Repeat with remaining apple slices. Sprinkle the raviolis with the cinnamon and dehydrate for 3 -8 hours at 118F (45c) degrees.

Serving Suggestions: top with sweet Ricotta cheese (page 22), fresh fruit and edible flowers.

Deluxe Fruit Cracker

1 1/2 cups dry golden flax seeds
1 1/4 cup water
1 tablespoon maple syrup
1/4 cup fresh or frozen raspberries
1 tablespoon fresh cranberries
2 tablespoons of yellow or other raisin
2 tablespoons currents
2 tablespoons chopped almonds

Put flax seeds in large bowl with maple syrup and 3/4 cup of the water. After an hour and a half add the remaining water and stir well. Stir in remaining ingredients and spread thinly on dehydrator sheet. Dehydrate for 2 hours at 118F (45c). Remove, flip onto mesh sheet and dehydrate another 5 hours.

Brotwurst
Spreadable sausage substitute by Cara "Brot"man

2 servings
1 cup walnuts, soaked for an hour then drained
1 cup almonds, soaked for an hour then drained
3 carrots
1 tablespoon fresh beet (for color)

2 tablespoons Braggs liquid amino's
1/2 cup savory cream (page 18)
1 tablespoon olive oil
1/2 cup minced parsley
Salt and pepper to taste

Put first 4 ingredients through Champion or twin gear juicer or put in food processor till well ground. Add to food processor with remaining ingredients. Process until somewhat creamy. Mold into a tube shape.
Serving suggestions: Stir in tablespoon of cream after blending in blender with minced onion and sliced tomato with a cracker on the side.

To make into actual sausage, see the video at Brotwurst.com

Appetizers

Endive Boats
Makes 3 endive boats

3 large endive leaves
3 tablespoons favorite hummus
1/2 cucumber cut into 1/3 slices
1/2 tomato, chopped
2 tablespoons purple onion, thinly chopped
1/2 an avocado, cubed
few mint leaves, torn
drizzle of lemon
drizzle of olive oil
salt & pepper to taste

Gently peel 3 leaves off endive. Spread 1 tablespoon of the hummus evenly on each leaf. Top with remaining ingredients & finish w lemon, oil, salt & pepper

Spring Rolls
Yields 2 rolls

2 coconut wrappers

Filling
1/2 cup thinly sliced purple cabbage
1/2 cup zucchini pasta (page 154)
1/2 cup loosely packed cilantro leaves
1/4 cup fresh mint leaves
4 basil leaves, torn
1 tablespoons chopped red pepper
1 green onion, thinly sliced

Drain liquid well from "pasta" and place in bowl with remaining ingredients. Stir everything together, then lay about 3 tablespoons evenly across lower portion of coconut wrapper. Roll up tightly and cut in half. Repeat with next roll. Serve with dipping sauce.

Dipping Sauce:
1/2 cup Cashew Butter
1 1/4 tablespoon maple syrup
2 tablespoons Nama Shoyu
1 1/2 tablespoon orange juice
1 1/2 tablespoons lime juice
1 tablespoon toasted sesame oil
1 tablespoon minced ginger
1/2 tablespoon minced garlic
Place all ingredients in a bowl and whisk together till creamy & smooth.

Jalapeño Poppers

Makes 1/2 dozen poppers

3 red or green jalapeño peppers
1 cup cashew cheese
1/2 teaspoon cumin powder
1 tablespoon water
1/2 cup cilantro
1 cup flax powder
1 tablespoon olive oil

Cut jalapeños evenly in half and scrape out the pith and seeds, set aside. Add cumin water and cilantro to cheese and stir. If cheese is too thick, add a little water. Stuff each jalapeño with a little of the cheese then cover in flax crumbs. Place on dehydrator sheet and drizzle each popper with olive oil. Dehydrate for 4 hours.

Breakfast

unBacon & unEggs with unHashBrowns
Serves 2

Ok, we had to do this just to show its possible. It may not be an everyday thing, but will definitely get some raised eyebrows and smiles from people.

unBacon: page 32

unEgg: 1 cup fresh coconut meat, blended. Yolk is 1 small orange tomato, cut in half,

Hash browns:
4 cups shredded zucchini, pressed w/ clean cloth to remove water
mix with 1 cup cashew butter

Form patties and put in dehydrator
1 or 2 hours later, brush on low sodium tamari, soy sauce or nama shoyu
Dehydrate overnight

Breakfast sausage: use pepperoni mix (page 184)

Banana Pancakes
(not pictured here. Image on page 196) Makes 8 mini pancakes

1 1/2 large ripe bananas
1 1/2 cups coconut cream (page 18)
1/2 cup coconut meat
1/4 cup flax ground up flax seeds
1/2 cup chopped walnuts
1/2 cup frozen blueberries
Put all ingredients except nuts and berries in food processor or blender and blend till smooth. Stir in berries and nuts, and pour out onto dehydrator sheet and form pancakes. Dehydrate for 3 hours on 118F (45c) or until able to flip onto mesh screen. Continue dehydrating another 5 hrs or until all liquid is dry.

SERVING SUGGESTION: Top with sweet cream (page 18), sliced strawberries, candied nuts & maple syrup.

Breakfast Fruit Salads

Mixed fresh seasonal fruit
cashew milk (page 18)

Toppings:
Cacao nibs, dried mulberries that have been dehydrated even crunchier, slivered almonds, pomegranate powder, chia, etc

We make these a lot

Oatmeal W/ Fruit
1 serving

1 cup oat groats soaked overnight in good water.
1/4 cup cashew milk (page 18) plus extra
splash vanilla
fruit for garnish

Drain and rinse groats and add to blender with 1/4 cup of milk. Pulse 3 times and pour into cereal bowl. Pour 2 tablespoons of milk into bowl.

Suggested toppings: Fresh and dried fruit, nuts

Breakfast Crisps with Cashew Butter, Mango, Banana

1 mango
1 banana
cashew butter
coconut flakes
flax cracker (page 36)

Put mango flesh in blender or food processor a few seconds, or until flesh just starts to become creamy. Cut banana in 1/2 inch squares. Smear cashew butter over cracker, top with mango, then banana and coconut flakes.

SERVING SUGGESTION: Serve on fruit cracker (page 36). Drizzle some sweet cream on it made from whisking a little maple syrup and cashew butter real well.

Edible Flower pictured: Garden Mum

Curry Omelet
Serves 2

1 1/2 cups coconut meat
1/4 teaspoon curry powder
1/4 teaspoon salt
1/2 teaspoon onion powder
1/2 teaspoon fresh thyme
1/2 teaspoon nutritional yeast
1/3 teaspoon turmeric
1 teaspoon Nama Shoyu
1 to 2 teaspoons coconut water

Place all ingredients in blender except for 1 teaspoon of coconut water and blend on high till smooth. If a little thick add 2nd teaspoon of coconut water. Pour on dehydrator sheet in approximately 3 x 4 inch pancake. Dehydrate for 3 hours or until dry enough to flip upside down and transfer onto dehydrator mesh sheet. Dehydrate for another hour or until the consistency of scrambled eggs.

Yogurt Sauce
1 teaspoon white miso
2 teaspoon cashew butter
1 tablespoon fresh lemon juice
1 tablespoon of olive oil
1/2 cup cream (page 18)
1 teaspoon minced cilantro
1 teaspoon minced mint

SERVING SUGGESTION: After blending stir in dehydrated red pepper, onion & mushroom before putting in dehydrator.

See video at CurryOmelete.com

Edible Flower pictured: Purslane (Portulaca)

Durian Custard w/ Fruit
Serves 2

1 1/2 cups durian flesh
1 durian seed
meat from 1 young Thai coconut
2 tablespoons fresh squeezed lemon or lime juice (grate rinds for garnish later)
1 teaspoon coconut water
splash vanilla

Add all ingredients to blender and blend on high for 10 seconds. If cream is too thick drizzle in a little bit more coconut water. Top with fruit.

SERVING SUGGESTION: Top with dried and fresh fruit, candied or regular nuts, cacao nibs, raspberry sauce (3/4 thawed raspberries blended in blender than put in squeeze jar), cashew milk.

Shown drizzled with Chocolate Syrup (page 36)

Edible Flowers pictured: Garden Mum

Cleansing Breakfast

The term "breakfast" means breaking your fast. Sleep is a form of fasting, where your body has a chance to rest and not eat or digest. It's not wise to start the day with a huge heavy breakfast, we should ease into it and max out our heavy stuff later during the day. Liquids are great for mornings. We often just do drinks like green smoothies, or fruit with cashew milk.

Some days all we want is what you see in this picture- some lemon water and grapes. They are very cleansing to the body. We feel light and clean. It doesn't take much to run a body when it's clean and working right.

I have breakfast at 12 noon and Cara doesn't eat anything until around 2 or 3 in the afternoon. This is called "Intermittent Fasting", meaning the body is fasting/cleansing for 16 hours every day and we eat for no more than 8 hours a day. Try it some time. Watch our video on intemittent fasting at MarkusNews.com

Veggie Sushi with Caviar Lime (not real caviar)

Lunch

unTuna Salad
2 servings

1 cup lightly packed (soaked for half hour and drained) sunflower seeds.
1 celery stick, thinly sliced
3 tablespoons minced onions
1/4 teaspoon salt
1 1/2 tablespoons mayo (and more for lettuce leaf)
1 teaspoon cilantro or your favorite herb (mint, parsley, dill,basil)
3/4 tablespoon lemon juice
1/2 teaspoon apple cider vinegar
1 red leaf lettuce leaf
1 favorite pickle spear

Salt and pepper to taste
Pulse chop sunflower seeds in food processor for 5 seconds. Stop, open and scrape down sides of canister. Process for 3 more seconds then add to bowl and stir in next 7 ingredients. Put a dollop of the mayo on a lettuce leaf and half the tuna. Serve with a pickle

Topping Suggestions: Pickled ginger, tomato, more onion, garlic, avocado, olive or truffle oil, nutritional yeast.

Mayonaise

1teaspoon light or yellow miso
2 teaspoon cashew butter
1 tablespoon lemon juice
1 tablespoon olive oil
Add all ingredients except olive oil to bowl and whisk till smooth. Slowly drizzle oil in while whisking with other hand. Whisk well a few times.

See video at UnTuna.com

Edible Flower pictured: Mum

unChicken Tacos

Guacamole
2 medium avocados, mashed
1/2 cup loosely packed finely chopped cilantro
1/4 cup finely minced purple onion
2 tablespoons lime juice
3/4 teaspoon salt
1 teaspoon finely minced jalapeño
Add all ingredients to a bowl and stir very well.

Flax Seed Taco
1 cup golden flax
1 cup good water
1 teaspoon onion powder
Add all ingredients to bowl, stir well and let sit. After an hour if mixture is thick add a little bit more water while stirring. Pour about 1/3 cup of batter onto dehydrator sheet and with offset spatula spread out into a circle. After 2 hours flip onto dehydrator mesh sheet. If you have a taco mold after an hour you can slip it in there and put a scrunched up piece of paper between the shell so the tops don't dry closed. Dehydrate a couple more hours or until crispy.

Filling
2 oyster mushrooms
1 teaspoon olive oil
pinch salt & pepper
1/2 cup thinly sliced white cabbage

Pull apart oyster mushrooms to make 1/2 inch wide shreds. Put in bowl and coat with oil. Place on dehydrator sheet, sprinkle with salt and pepper and dehydrate 2 hours. Make avocado cream sauce.

Avocado Cream Sauce
1 medium avocado
2 tablespoons lime juice
1/2 cup good water
1/2 teaspoon salt
2 tablespoon savory cream
Blend in blender until smooth or mash with fork

Spread a little of the guacamole across inside of taco shell. Add cabbage, mock chicken (oyster mushrooms) and guacamole. Drizzle with avocado cream sauce on top.

Pumpkin Ravioli
Makes 1 dozen

1 butternut squash
1 tablespoon olive oil
pinch salt & pepper
1 cup pine nuts
1/2 cup cashews (unsoaked)
1/4 cup nutritional yeast
1 tablespoon lemon juice
1 tablespoon Braggs liquid amino's
1/2 cup plus 2 tablespoons water

1/2 Teaspoon thyme
Pinch salt & pepper

Peel butternut squash and slice very fine on mandolin. If slices come out too thin just make full wrapper by overlapping them. They'll stick together in the end. Brush a dehydrator sheet generously with olive oil and lay butternut squash circles in one layer across sheet. Sprinkle with salt & pepper and dehydrate for 45 minutes or until soft. Add the next 4 ingredients to blender. Add 2/3 cup of the water and blend on high till smooth. Add remaining water and blend for 3 seconds. When squash are soft, place a small dollop of the cashew cheese in the center of squash circle and cover with another slice. Gently press the edges together and repeat. Lay out on sheet individually and brush with more oil. Sprinkle with fresh thyme, salt & pepper. Dehydrate for 1 1/2 to 4 hours.

SERVING SUGGESTION: Sprinkle with red pepper flakes, minced parsley, minced garlic, dehydrated mushroom and herbs. Drizzle of truffle oil. Top with caramelized onions. Caramelize onions by thinly slicing one onion on mandolin and coating well in olive oil. Sprinkle with salt & pepper. Lay out on dehydrator sheet and dehydrate for 5 hours.

Naan Wrap
Makes 1

1 naan (page 24)
unbacon (page 34)
3 tomato slices
1 onion slice
pinch cilantro
favorite sprout

Smear a little dipping sauce across naan. Lay out all ingredients on naan. Fold into a wrap and serve w/ wrap dipping sauce.

Wrap Dipping Sauce
2 tablespoons cashew butter
2 tablespoons lemon juice
1 tablespoon tahini
1 tablespoon good water
3 tablespoons olive oil
Place all ingredients but oil in bowl and whisk till smooth. Slowly drizzle oil while whisking.

Coconut Wrap
Makes 2 wraps

2 cups coconut meat
4 tablespoons coconut water
1/3 teaspoon sea salt

Add coconut meat to blender and blend on high for 5 seconds. Add coconut water and blend 15 seconds.
Pour out half of blender contents onto dehydrator sheet. Spread evenly 1/4 inch thick with off set spatula. Repeat. Dehydrate for 2 hours on 118. Remove, flip onto mesh screen and dehydrate another hour and a half then begin checking for doneness. Should be pliable and show no signs of liquid.

Reuben
Serves 1

1 burger patty page 28
2 slices cheese of choice: page 22 or 26
1 beautiful red leaf lettuce
2 slices purple onion cut thin
2 slices tomato
2 tablespoons sauerkraut
1 pickle spear cut in half

Thousand Island Dressing
1 cup coconut meat
3/4 cup apple cider vinegar
1/3 cup fresh tomato
1/3 cup olive oil
3 tablespoons sun dried tomato
3 tablespoons pine nuts
2 tablespoons MarkusSweet
1 teaspoon sea salt
1/2 teaspoon onion powder
1/e teaspoon paprika
pinch cayenne

1/3 cucumber

Blend everything but cucumber in blender until smooth.
Chop 1/3 cucumber in food processor into relish-sized bits and drain. Mix in with sauce.

SERVING SUGGESTION: Drizzle a few drops of truffle oil across Reuben. Top with caramelized onions. Caramelize onions by thinly slicing one onion on mandolin and coating well in olive oil. Sprinkle with salt & pepper. Dehydrate at 118F (45c) for 5 hours, prior to assembling Reuben.

Dinner

Kung Pao Chicken
Serves 2

"Meat"
3/4 cup coconut meat

1/2 teaspoon paprika
1/4 teaspoon chipotle powder

Cut larger pieces of coconut meat into 1 by 1 (roughly) pieces/squares and marinate in bowl with sauce (below) overnight in refrigerator, then place on dehydrator sheet. Rub paprika and chipotle powder on coconut and dehydrate for at least 3 hrs.

Sauce
3 tablespoons Nama Shoyu (raw soy sauce)
1 teaspoon minced ginger
5 tablespoons water
2 tablespoons toasted sesame oil
1 teaspoon lime juice
1/4 teaspoon five spice
1 tablespoon sun dried tomatoes
1/2 teaspoon maple syrup
1 Teaspoon apple cider vinegar
1/2 teaspoon onion powder
pinch paprika

Place all ingredients in blender and blend for 2 minutes, set aside.

Chinese Salad
1 cup thinly sliced white cabbage
1/2 cup chopped cilantro
1/4 red pepper, cut into spears
1/2 cup scallions finely sliced
1 tablespoon cashews

To bowl add Chinese Salad ingredients. Top with some mock chicken pieces then pour sauce on top. For rice, use parsnip rice from Indian Feast recipe on next page.

Indian Feast (Naan recipe on page 24)
Serves 2

Tomato Masala
3 cups tomatoes on the vine, thinly sliced
2 cups white onion, cut in half then cut into 1/4 inch slices
2 tablespoons olive oil
2 garlic cloves, minced
1 tablespoon ginger, minced
1/2 teaspoon ground coriander
1 teaspoon ground cumin
1/3 teaspoon ground cardamom (if you don't have all these spices don't sweat it!)
1/3 teaspoon nutmeg
1/2 teaspoon paprika
1/3 teaspoon cayenne powder
Add all ingredients to a large bowl and toss well to coat tomatoes. Pour onto dehydrator sheet. Scrape everything off sheet onto tomatoes. Dehydrate at 118 for 3 1/2 hours. Fold dehydrator sheet and slide tomato contents into bowl. Add a tablespoon of the cilantro & mint raiter and stir.

Parsnip and jicama rice (Process parsnip and jicama separately)
1 cup parsnip rice (pulse chopped parsnips in food processor till size of rice)
1 tablespoon cashew butter
Salt and pepper to taste. Optional: add 1 tablespoon cilantro and 1 tablespoon Nama Shoyu.
Combine parsnip and cashew butter, salt and pepper and mix well till "rice" sticks together.

Cilantro and Mint Raiter
1 cup loosely packed cilantro
1 cup loosely packed mint
1 cup cashew cream
1 teaspoon lemon juice
1/4 teaspoon curry powder
1/4 teaspoon cumin powder
1/4 teaspoon chaat masala (optional)
Grind cilantro & mint (coffee grinder works)
add to bowl
add cream, lemon and spices and stir to blend.
1 teaspoon minced mint

Yogurt Sauce
1 teaspoon white miso
2 teaspoon cashew butter
1 tablespoon fresh lemon juice
1 tablespoon of olive oil
1/2 cup cream
1 teaspoon minced cilantro
1 teaspoon minced mint

Serve a small portion of each dish to plate.

Spicy Thai Curry Noodle UnChicken
One Serving

1 cup coconut meat from young Thai coconut

MARINADE
3 tablespoons Nama Shoyu (raw soy sauce)
1 red minced chili pepper
1/2 teaspoon grated lime zest
2 tablespoons lime juice
2 tablespoons olive oil
1/2 teaspoon toasted sesame oil (optional)
1 1/2 tablespoons finely minced lemon grass (now available in most produce departments' "fresh herbs" section)
1 tablespoon minced ginger
1/4 teaspoon curry powder
 1 garlic clove minced

Toppings
1/2 cup cilantro
1 tablespoon chopped basil
1 tablespoon chopped mint
1 garlic clove minced (optional)

To large bowl add all marinade ingredients and lightly whisk and set aside. Cut larger pieces of coconut meat into 1 by 1 (roughly) pieces/squares and add to marinade. Toss well to coat and pour onto dehydrator sheet. Scrape the bowl of all the marinade onto sheet and slide into dehydrator for 2 hours.
Remove from dehydrator and scrape everything into serving bowl. Add toppings, combine and serve with wedge of lime.

SERVING SUGGESTION: Serve with either zuchini noodles on next page or side of parsnip rice (1 cup chopped parsnip to food processor processed till rice size.
1 teaspoon cashew butter mixed in well. Salt & pepper to taste.

Edible Flower pictured: Hibiscus

Pasta in Cream Sauce
Serves 2

Pasta
4 zucchinis
1 teaspoon olive oil
pinch salt

Peel zucchini and thinly slice on mandolin linguini style. Put dry pasta into bowl and drizzle oil and salt on top. Stir up pasta by hand, ensuring oil and salt are evenly coating zucchini then set aside for 45 minutes. Make cream sauce.

Cream Sauce
1 cup pine nuts
1/2 cup soaked cashews
1/4 cup nutritional yeast
1 tablespoon lemon juice
1 tablespoon Braggs liquid amino's
1/2 cup plus 2 tablespoons good water

Add all ingredients but last one to blender. Add 2/3 cup of the water and blend on high till smooth. Add remaining water and blend for 2 seconds. Pour over pasta.

SERVING SUGGESTIONS: Top w/ minced garlic, fresh parsley, ground pepper, nutritional yeast and truffle or olive oil

See video at HealthyCremePasta.com

Spicy Thai Cabbage
Serves 5

(in bowl)
1/2 red cabbage, chopped
1 cup cashews
1 1/2 cups scallions
2 cups cilantro, chopped
1 1/2 cup golden raisins
1 teaspoon sea salt
top with 1/2 cup apple cider vinegar
2 tablespoons sesame oil
2 tablespoons toasted sesame oil
Mix

Mix in little side bowl until smooth:
1/2 cup cashew butter
1/4 cup apple cider vinegar
4 tablespoons toasted sesame oil
1 teaspoon hot chili oil

Pour over big mixing bowl, mix everything

Eat that day if you can. Best if not refrigerated (the oils get hard and white).
Will keep overnight unrefrigerated.

You can see the video at MarkusNews.com

Mango Blueberry Mint
Serves 2-3

Words cannot explain the taste explosion in your mouth when you eat this

4 cups mango, cubed
3 cups blueberries
3/4 of a jalapeño pepper, finely chopped
3-4 cloves garlic, finely chopped
1 1/2 tablespoons finely chopped ginger
1/2 cup mint leaves, finely chopped
juice of 1 lime
1/2 teaspoon sea salt

You can see the video online at MangoGarlic.com

Pasta Pomodoro
Serves 2

Pasta
4 zucchini
1 tablespoon olive oil
1/2 teaspoon salt
Peel zucchini and thinly slice on mandolin linguini style. Put dry pasta into large bowl and drizzle oil and salt on top. Gently stir up pasta with your hand ensuring oil and salt are evenly coating zucchini then set aside for 45 minutes while pasta "cooks". The longer they sit the more pasta like they become. Lasts 2 days in fridge.

Sauce
3 cups cherry tomatoes, cut in half
3 tablespoons olive oil
2 garlic cloves, minced
1 teaspoon fresh lime or lemon juice
1 teaspoon fresh thyme, minced
3 basil leaves, torn
salt and pepper to taste

Throw everything in a large bowl & mix well. Lay out onto dehydrator sheet and dehydrate at 118 for 3 hours or until soft & flavors have blended. Use tongs (or hands) to lift a serving of pasta from bowl and onto serving plate. Scoop up a half cup of the tomatoes and sauce and put on top of pasta. Sprinkle w/ a little nutritional yeast on top.

Garnish: Onion rings (page 32) Ricotta cheese (page 74)

Thai Curry Noodles
Serves 2

1 cup pasta
3/4 cup thinly sliced purple cabbage
2 green onions, quarter inch sliced
1/2 red pepper, quarter inch slices
1/2 cup mint, torn
1/2 cup basil, torn
1/2 cup cilantro, chopped
1 coconut wrapper, sliced to noodle shape (optional)
Combine above ingredients in a large bowl. Add to serving bowls. Make dressing.

Dressing:
1/2 cup cashew cheese recipe
1 1/4 tablespoon maple syrup
2 tablespoons Nama Shoyu
1 tablespoon orange juice
1 1/2 tablespoons lime juice
1/2 teaspoon toasted sesame oil
1/4 teaspoon curry powder
1 tablespoon minced ginger
1/2 tablespoon minced garlic
Place all ingredients in a bowl and whisk together till creamy & smooth. Drizzle over noodles.

Tropical Salsa
Serves 3

The buttery smooth taste sensation of this salad makes it a regular Markus favorite.

2 cups mango, cubed
2 cups papaya, cubed
1 cup red onion, cubed
1/4 cup olive oil
1/4 cup apple cider vinegar
1 1/2 cups cilantro, chopped
1/2 teaspoon sea salt
pinch of black pepper

Mix

Use meat of 2 avocados to create a flower design as a bed for the salad.
Top with the colorful mixture from above. Be sure to take a bite of avocado with each bite.

You can see the video online at TropicalSalsa.com

Tomato, Ricotta & Mushroom Pizza
Serves 3

For Crust
3/4 cup golden flax seed
3/4 cup good water
Put flax in bowl & cover w water. Soak for 1 hour.
2 cups carrot pulp
1 1/2 tablespoons sun dried tomatoes, minced
1/2 cup purple onion, 1/4 inch slices
1 tablespoon Nama Shoyu
Put all ingredients in a large bowl. If flax is firm add a little more water & stir well.
Add to pulp bowl and stir very well ensuring everything is well incorporated. Pour out onto dehydrator sheet and spread 1/4 - 1/2 thick w/ offset spatula. Dehydrate for 3 hours then flip onto mesh sheet. Cut into triangle shaped slices at this point if desired. Dehydrate another 3 hours or until crisp.

Topping
1 1/2 cups thinly sliced heirloom to vine ripened tomato
1 cup white onion, sliced in 1/4 inch slices
1/2 teaspoon thyme
1 garlic clove, minced
1 tablespoon curly parsley, finely minced
1 tablespoon olive oil
1/4 teaspoon salt
Put everything in a large bowl and toss well to coat. Lay out on dehydrator sheet & dehydrate for 3 hours or until flavors have melded and onions are soft.

Ricotta Cheese
See feta cheese recipe under Greek Salad

Assembly
Smear a layer of the ricotta cheese evenly all over crust. Top with tomatoes and onions and it's juices, sliced mushroom and ricotta cheese dollops.
Sprinkle w fresh curly minced parsley.

Vegetables Vesuvio Over Noodles
Serves 3

2 cups tomato quartered 1/2 inch width
3 scallions, chopped in 1 inch pieces
1 cup zucchini, sliced in 1/2 inch circles
1 celery stick, chopped in half inch pieces
1 cup shiitaki, crimini or portabello mushroom, cut in bite size squares
1 cup onion quartered 1/2 width
1/4 cup chopped carrot
1 red pepper, roughly chopped into 1 by 1 inch squares
3 garlic cloves, roughly chopped
3 tablespoons olive oil
1 teaspoon fresh thyme
Fennel leaf (optional)
1/2 cup chopped parsley
1 teaspoon fresh oregano
1/2 tablespoon salt
1/2 tablespoon pepper

Add all ingredients to a large bowl and toss well to coat. Lay out evenly in one layer on dehydrator sheet scraping all the contents out of bowl onto tomatoes. Dehydrate at 1118F (45c) for 5 1/2 hours. Serve with zucchini pasta.

vegetables used

Barley on the Half Shell
Serves 1

1 cup barley, soaked for 5 hours
3 broccoli florets, cut small
2 tablespoons tomatoes, chopped small
1 tablespoon red pepper, diced
1/2 green onion, chopped small
1/2 celery stalk, sliced thin
1/4 an avocado, sliced
1 tablespoon purple onion, thinly sliced

Add everything to bowl and toss. Top w/ sauce

Sauce
2 teaspoon white miso
4 teaspoon cashew butter
2 tablespoon lemon juice
2 tablespoon olive oil
Add all ingredients except olive oil to bowl and whisk till smooth. Slowly drizzle oil in while whisking with other hand. Continue whisking for a few seconds to blend.

SERVING SUGGESTION: Top w/ pea sprouts, radishes, dill, a drizzle of truffle or olive oil

Now Thats'a Italiano!
Serves 3

The same pizza as page 166 but with dehydrated shiitaki mushrooms & fresh herbs

Sushi Nori
Makes 2 rolls

2 nori sheets (sushi wrappers)
1/2 cup feta cheese (see Greek Salad recipe)
1/4 avocado, cut into strips
1 strip of green onion, sliced length wise until thin strip
1/4 red or yellow pepper, cut into thin strips
1/2 cup spinach or other green
1/4 cup pineapple,sliced thin (optional)
1/4 cup Manitok wild rice, soaked overnight (optional)

Lay out one sheet on clean, dry wooden cutting board, smooth side down. Have a small container of water nearby to dip your fingers in to seal roll. Lay out a layer of dry spinach or other greens across the lower portion of sheet. Drop small pieces of feta cheese evenly on top of spinach going across roll. Neatly lay out one of each of the rest ingredients across roll and spread across roll with rice. Roll tightly and seal roll by dipping fingers in small container of water and running it along sushi roll seam to stick. Dip fingers and apply to any edges that didn't adhere. Repeat w/ remaining roll & serve w Nama Shoyu., pickled ginger &/or wasabi

For pickled ginger, marinate thin ginger slices in apple cider vinegar overnight.

Sushi Lite
Makes 2 rolls

1 decorative rice wrappers (sushi wrapper available in Asian section at Whole Foods)
1/2 cup spinach, sprouts or favorite green
2 tablespoons feta cheese (see Greek salad for recipe)
3 tablespoons kale chips (page 92)
1 strip of green onion, sliced length wise until thin strip
1/4 avocado
1/4 red or yellow pepper, cut into thin strips
1/2 cup spinach or other green
1/4 cup pineapple, sliced thin (optional)
1/2 cup quinoa, soaked and sprouted for a couple days (optional)

Lay out one sheet on clean, dry wooden cutting board, smooth side of sushi wrapper down. Have a small container of water nearby to dip your fingers in to seal roll. Lay out a layer of dry greens or other greens across the lower portion of sheet making sure to bring it all the way to the edge or you'll have air pockets in your roll. Drop small pieces of feta cheese evenly on top of spinach going across roll. Next lay kale evenly across. Neatly lay out one of each of the rest ingredients across roll. Roll tightly and seal roll by dipping fingers in small container of water and running it along sushi roll seam to stick. Repeat w/ remaining roll & serve w Nama Shoyu., pickled ginger &/or wasabi.

Edible Flower pictured: Hibiscus

Nigiri
Makes 2

Its mind blowing how much this feels and tastes like raw fish!

1 nori sheet, cut into 1 inch wide strips
1 aloe vera leaf
1/2 cup purple beet juice
1 green onion, thinly sliced

Cut skin off Aloe vera and cut the gel into 1 by 2 inch pieces. While running under cold water massage aloe till no longer slippery. This will also release a lot of the bitter from the aloe. Marinate in beet juice for 15 minutes, rinse and pat dry.

Rice
1 cup parsnip
1 tablespoon cashew butter

Pulse chop parsnip in food processor until size of rice. Combine parsnip and cashew butter, and mix well until "rice" sticks together. Form rice rectangle, lay red-staind aloe piece on top and wrap a nori strip. Place on plate seal side down with a side of Nama Shoyu.

Soak thinly sliced ginger in apple cider vinegar overnight and add as garnish

See video at RawVeganSushi.com

Gourmet Lasagna
Serves 2

Tomato Filling

2 cups large heirloom, or other tomato
2 large garlic cloves, minced
spreadable.
1 white onion, finely minced
2 tablespoons parsley, finely minced
2 basil leaves, torn
2 tablespoons olive oil
1 teaspoon fresh thyme
1/2 teaspoon salt
Slice tomatoes into 1/4 inch circles.
Place all in bowl with remaining ingredients,
toss well to coat. Scrape everything out
onto a dehydrator sheet and dehydrate at 118F (45c) for 4-5 hours.

Ricotta Filling

Use cheese recipe from page 74 and add
2 tablespoons water to make it

Mix following ingredients into cheese mix:
1 tablespoon green onion, minced
2 tablespoons curly parsley, finely minced
1 garlic clove, finely minced
1/2 teaspoon cracked pepper corn
1/4 teaspoon salt
1/3 teaspoon nutmeg (optional)

Pasta

4 zucchini, as fat as possible
2 teaspoons olive oil
1/3 teaspoon salt
Wash & peel zucchini. Thinly (as possible) slice one side of zucchini on mandolin stopping
at the seeds. Flip zucchini over, peel other side stopping at the seeds. Put away seeded
part of zucchini. Put the zucchini strips in a wide casserole style dish. Drizzle the oil &
sprinkle salt evenly all over strips then gently toss to coat some more and set aside for 25
minutes to "cook".

Assembly

Take a zucchini strip and lay vertically 3/4 inch off center of serving plate. Take another
zucchini strip and lay it next to 1st strip slightly overlapping. Take another strip and place
overlapping 1st strips other side. Repeat with one more strip. Drop small pieces of ricotta
cheese all over the zucchini strips & gently spread evenly. Lay tomatoes w/ onions on
top of ricotta cheese layer being sure to include tomato drippings from dehydrator sheet.
Cover tomatoes w/ another layer of the zucchini strips layered out just like the first time. Add
ricotta, another layer of tomato and cover with one more layer of zucchini strips laid across
tomatoes. Garnish with basil leaf and more tomato drippings from the dehydrator tray.

Markus Pizza

This even has flexible crust just like real pizza! And the pepperonis- wow, just like the real thing. Once the crust is done, you can add the sauce and cheese etc and eat right away if you want, or dehydrate a few hours to harden cheese and condense sauce. 1 pizza makes 7 slices.

Pizza Crust (in blender)
2 cups coconut meat
1/2 cup coconut water
3/4 cup fresh onion
1/4 cup ground chia seeds
3 tablespoons nutritional yeast

Dehydrate 4 hrs, flip onto screen then dehydrate overnight

Pizza Cheese (in blender)
1 cup unsoaked cashews
1/4 cup pine nuts
1 tablespoon nutritional yeast
2 tablespoosn apple cider vinegar
pinch sea salt
1/2 cup water
1 teaspoon Italian seasoning

Pizza sauce (in blender)
1 cup sun dried tomatoes
1 cup fresh tomatoes
3 tablespoon cashew milk (page18)
1 teaspoon apple cider vinegar
1 teaspoon olive oil
2 dates
1 clove garlic
pinch sea salt
pinch of black pepper
pinch of cayenne

Pepperoni
1/2 cup coconut meat
1/3 cup Sea moss gel
2 tablespoons finely chopped sun dried tomatoes
1/4 cup finely chopped red bell pepper
1 tablespoon raisins, chopped into small bits
1/2 teasp fresh beet (see pic)
1 1/2 tablespoons Nama Shoyu or soy sauce

Chop coarsely in blender or food processor (see pic)
Make patties and dehydrate, flipping half way

Other possible toppings for pizza- pineapple, green onions, Sun dried tomato pieces, red onion

See video at IncrediPizza.com

Kids

Mac and Cheese

Noodles
Fresh coconut meat cut into strips, then chopped to rectangles

Cheese (blend)
1 cup cashews, unsoaked
2 tablespoons pine nuts
1 teaspoon nutritional yeast
1 teaspoon paprika
1/4v teaspoon turmeric
juice of half lemon
1/2 teaspoon sea salt
1/3 cup water
1 teaspoon apple cider vinegar
2 teaspoon maple syrup
1/4 cup coconut meat

See video at HealthyMacNCheese.com

Pop Tarts (makes 6)

Crust
2 cups coconut meat
2 cups almond meal (ground up almonds)
2 tablespoons maple syrup
3 cups water

Icing
1 1/2 cups coconut meat
4 tablespoons coconut butter
4 coconut blossom syrup or 3 tablespoons maple syrup
1 teaspoon vanilla

Filling
Raspberries, blended

Sprinkles
Red- dehydrated raspberries or goji berries, finely chopped
Yellow- dehydrated pineapple finely chopped
Orange- dehydrated mango, finely chopped

Smear dough thin and flat onto dehydrator sheets
Dehydrate 5 hours 6 hrs, flip onto screen dehydrate another 5-6 hours until center is not gooey anymore, but crust is still flexible

Cut into rectangles

Spread raspberry jam on one, icing on the other
Put two pieces together, add sprinkles on top

Can eat right away or dehydrate more to make "icing" harder.

See video at MarkusPopTarts.com

Spaghettios

Sauce (blender)
2 cups fresh tomatoes
2 cups Sun dried tomatoes (either dry ones soaked 2 hrs or those that come in olive oil)
2 cups water
2 teaspoons olive oil
2 teaspoons apple cider vinegar
4 dates
2 cloves garlic
1/4 teaspoon sea salt

Little Noodle bits
chopped zucchini strands (the middle piece left over from spiralizing)

Broccoli and Cheese

Marinate 2 cups broccoli in olive oil and a bit of sea salt and pepper, then dehydrate for 4 hours.

When ready to eat, take out of dehydrator so it's still warm and add the cheese (Same cheese as Mac and Cheese, page 188)

Cheese
1 cup cashews
2 tablespoons pine nuts
1 teaspoon nutritional yeast
1 teaspoon paprika
1/4v teaspoon turmeric
juice of half lemon
1/2 teaspoon sea salt
1/3 cup water
1 teaspoon apple cider vinegar
2 teaspoon maple syrup
1/4 cup coconut meat

Banana pancakes- recipe on page 122

Desserts

Crème Brûlée
2 Servings

Version 1:
1 1/2 cups cashews, soaked for an hour
3 Medjool dates (the softer ones)
1 teaspoon maple syrup
1/2 cup thicker cashew creme (page 18)
1/2 vanilla bean
Add ingredients to blender and blend on high till smooth. Add a little more cashew milk if too thick. Pour into dish, top with sweet crust and garnish with raspberry and mint leaf.

Version 2:
Use durian as the creme (see durian breakfast)

Sweet Crust Topping:
1 cup coconut meat
1/4 cup maple syrup

Pour round blobs onto teflex dehydrator sheet and dehydrate 8-10 hours, flipping over onto mesh screen half way. When hard, you can cut with scissors into perfect circle and place on top of creme in bowl.

Top with berries

See video at HealthyCremeBrulee.com

Edible Flower pictured: Garden Mum

Chocolate Tacos
Makes 3 tacos

1 1/2 cups dry golden flax seeds
3/4 cup water
1/4 cup chocolate syrup

Put flax seeds in large bowl with maple syrup and water. After an hour and a half add the chocolate syrup and stir well. Drop about 1/3 batter onto dehydrator sheet. With offset spatula spread out into circle. Repeat till batters gone. Dehydrate for 2 hours at 118F (45c). Remove, flip onto mesh sheet and dehydrate another 5 hours. At this point you can decorate your taco if you choose. I put some cashew cream in a squeeze bottle and made designs in one and outlined another. I also rubbed thawed raspberries on the first one. If using taco mold remove from dehydrator when still pliable, 4 hours dehydrating time, and slip onto taco mold. Dehydrate another 3 hours or until crispy. Fill with cashew cream or fresh fruit or whatever else you can think of!

Edible Flower pictured: Pansy

90 Second Chocolate Ice Cream
Serves 2

This soft serve wonder is super fast and easy

(in blender)
2 frozen bananas
2 tablespoons cacao powder
1 tablespoon lemon juice (optional)
1 teaspoon vanilla

Pound the Vitamix plunger really hard and fast down the corners to make sure it mixes

Eat immediately

See video at 90SecondiceCream.com

Cannoli
Makes 2

4 apples, fuji or honey crisp
1/2 cup coconut oil, melted

1 1/2 cups ricotta cheese (page 74)
3 tablespoons coconut or date sugar
1 cup chopped walnuts
1 tablespoon cacao nibs, roughly chopped
half of a vanilla bean (seeds only)

Peel apples and slice quarter inch thick on mandolin. Generously brush coconut oil onto dehydrator sheet and lay apple slices out, not overlapping. When tray is full brush the tops of each apple slice and dehydrate at 118 for 1 1/2 hours or until pliable. Remove tray and lay apple slices overlapping each other 4 apple slices long. Repeat this step 4 times till you have about a 4 inch square of overlapping apple slices. Brush any dry pieces with coconut oil and dehydrate for 2 more hours. Remove from dehydrator and wrap around a cannoli mold and gently lay on mesh sheet. Repeat this step with remaining squares then dehydrate till firm and able to hold own shape. Gently slide cannoli off mold and continue to dehydrate till crispy. Stuff with filling.
If creating shell is too much trouble you can easily just overlap 4 apple slices and put a couple dollops of cannoli cheese in center of dehydrated apple wheels. Tastes exactly the same but at a fraction of the work!

Chocolate Syrup
1 cup cacao powder
1/2 cup plus 1 tablespoon maple syrup
1/2 cup plus 2 tablespoons cashew milk (page 18)
splash vanilla
tiny pinch salt

Put all ingredients in blender and blend on high. Put in jar & refrigerate. Lasts 2 days.

Cheese and Crackers

Cheese

2 cups soaked cashews
1 cup packed Sea moss gel
1 cup water

Place cashews and Sea moss in blender with 3/4 cup of water and turn on high. Use blender tamper to help blend almonds. Only add more water if your having trouble blending. Mold into a shape. I used a small bowl. Cover with the following toppings: Fruit cracker, cacao nibs, dried apricot, golden raisins, currants, goji berries, chopped almonds.

Cracker from page 36.

Edible Flower pictured: Purslane (Portulaca)

Chocolate Crush Pie
Makes 1 small, two inch mini spring form pie

Crust
1 cup almonds or hazelnuts (unsoaked)
1 1/2 tablespoon coconut oil
2 1/2 tablespoon maple syrup
2 tablespoons carob powder
Put nuts into a food processor and pulse chop into little bits. Put in bowl with other ingredients and stir to mix very well. Brush a mini spring form pie pan (or other little dish) w/ coconut oil and press nuts into pan with your hands forming a very thin crust. So thin it's one more push away from cracking. It's optional to go up the sides or not. You can't see the inside of the pie after released from pan if you do bring crust up the sides of pan. Set aside.

Pie
Makes 1 small, two inch mini spring form pie
3/4 cup chocolate syrup (page 36)
1 cup avocado
1/2 cup maple syrup
1/3 cup Sea moss
1/2 teaspoon vanilla
1 cup nut milk (page 18)

Add all ingredients to blender or food process and blend till smooth. Pour into pie crust. Top w/ grated orange and pop in freezer for half hour then move to fridge.

Chocolate Mousse
serves 2

Mousse
1 cup chocolate syrup (page 36)
1/2 cup avocado
1 tablespoon maple syrup
1 lid full vanilla flavoring
1 cup cashew milk (page 18)

Put all ingredients in blender & blend on high using tamper to help turn contents over. Use fruit cookie as crust or take about a tablespoon of the carob crust and form a flat circle. Place on plate & cover w/ a dollop of the mousse then a small dollop of whip cream (whip cream is cashew milk w/ less water). Make pretty designs with chocolate & raspberry in squeeze bottle.

Crust pictured is cookie from page 98)

Suggested crust:
1 cup brazil nuts
1 1/2 tablespoon coconut oil
2 1/2 tablespoon maple syrup
2 tablespoons carob powder

Put Brazil nuts into a food processor and pulse chop for 3 seconds three times. You want nuts to be in small pieces but not powdered at all. Pour into bowl with remaining crust ingredients. Pull out any large pieces of nut that barely touched the blade and chop yourself into tiny pieces, then put in bowl with other ingredients and stir to mix very well.

SUGGESTED TOPPINGS: Blueberries, cacao nibs, pomegranate seeds, chopped almonds, shredded coconut, mint leaf.

Fruit Crepe
Makes approximately 2 crepes

1 1/2 cups coconut meat
3/4 cup cashew milk (page 18)
1 teaspoon maple syrup or MarkusSweet
1 teaspoon vanilla

Blend all ingredients until smooth. Split batter on 2 dehydrator sheets to spread out in a large thin circle. Dehydrate on 118F (45c) for 2 hours. Take out and flip onto mesh sheet and dehydrate for another 2 hours or until completely dry and pliable. Fill with fruit, roll up tightly and dollop with sweet cream (page 18).

SERVING SUGGESTIONS: Garnish with sauce bowl of strawberry syrup by grinding up a cup of frozen then thawed strawberries in the blender till smooth. Or serve w/ side of chocolate syrup.

See video at HealthyCrepeRecipe.com

Cheesecake
Serves 2

Crust
1 cup almonds or hazelnuts
1 teaspoon cashew butter

Put nuts into a food processor and pulse chop for 4 seconds three times. Pour into bowl with cashew butter. Put in bowl with other ingredients and stir to mix very well. Brush a mini spring form pie pan (or other little dish) w/ coconut oil and press nuts into pan with your hands forming a very thin crust. So thin it's one more push away from cracking. It's optional to go up the sides or not. You can't see the inside of the pie after released from pan if you do bring crust up the sides of pan. Set aside.

Filling
1 cup coconut
3/4 cups cashews (unsoaked)
3 tablespoons maple syrup
1/2 cup coconut water
1 lid full vanilla flavor

Put all the filling ingredients in blender and blend on high till creamy smooth. Pour into mini pie pan. Put in freezer to set for 25 minutes then let chill in fridge for 4 hours before serving.

SERVING SUGGESTIONS: Drizzle raspberry sauce on plate before placing pie on it. Dried pineapple(shown), cacao nibs, strawberries, blueberries, shredded coconut, grated orange rind(shown), mint leaf(shown).

See video at RawVeganCheesecake.com

Pink Passion Pie

Crust
1 cup almonds or hazelnuts
1 teaspoon cashew butter

Put nuts into a food processor and pulse chop for 4 seconds three times. Pour into bowl with cashew butter. Put in bowl with other ingredients and stir to mix very well. Brush a mini spring form pie pan (or other little dish) w/ coconut oil and press nuts into pan with your hands forming a very thin crust. So thin it's one more push away from cracking. It's optional to go up the sides or not. You can't see the inside of the pie after released from pan if you do bring crust up the sides of pan. Set aside.

Pink Filling
1 cup coconut meat
1/4 cup maple syrup
2 tablespoons coconut oil
1/2 cup chopped beet
1 teaspoon vanilla

Blend all ingredients till smooth. Pour into pie pan and place in freezer to firm up for half hour. When firm, spread a layer of **sweet cream (page 18)** evenly over the pink mixture. Gently spoon the fruit mixture over cream and let pie firm in freezer for a couple hours. Let stand for 10 minutes after removing from freezer.

Fruit Mixture
2 tablespoons finely chopped apple
2 tablespoons finely chopped strawberries
1 kiwi, finely chopped
1 tablespoon fresh orange juice
seeds from 1/2 a pomegranate (optional)
1 tablespoon chopped walnut
Mix in bowl and set aside.

Garnish
Orange zest, candied almonds, pomegranate seeds, frozen raspberries
raspberry sauce (put one bag of thawed raspberries in blender & blend on high for 6 seconds. Pour into a squeeze bottle & drizzle over pie.

Edible Flower pictured: Dianthus

Fruit Leather Crepe

Throw a bunch of 80% thawed frozen raspberries in blender, pour on dehydrator sheet Flip after a few hours when top gets hard.

This fruit leather by itself is a great travel food.

As a desert crepe, fill with sweet cream from page 18 and fruit.

Chocolate Syrup

1 cup cacao powder
1/2 cup plus 1 tablespoon maple syrup
1/2 cup plus 2 tablespoons cashew milk (page 18)
splash vanilla
tiny pinch salt
Put all ingredients in blender and blend on high. Put in jar & refrigerate. Lasts 2 days.

Coconut Cream Flan W/ Pineapple Filling

Crust

1 cup brazil nuts
1 tablespoon coconut oil
1 tablespoon maple syrup

Put brazil nuts into a food processor and pulse chop for 4 seconds three times. You want nuts to be in very small pieces but not powdered at all. Pour into bowl with maple syrup & coconut oil. Pull out any large pieces of nut that barely touched the blade and chop yourself into tiny pieces, then put in bowl with other ingredients and stir to mix very well. Brush a mini (heart shaped) spring form pie pan (or other little dish) w/ coconut oil and press Brazil nuts into pan with your hands forming a very thin crust. So thin it's one more push away from cracking. It's optional to go up the sides or not. You can't see the inside of the pie after released from pan if you do bring crust up the sides of pan. Set aside.

Filling

1 cup tightly packed coconut meat
3/4 cup coconut water
 1/2 Cup Sea moss Gel
1/4 cup maple syrup
Splash vanilla
1/4 ripe pineapple, cored then cut into thin slices

Place first 4 ingredients (not the pineapple) in blender and blend for 20 seconds or until all blended and creamy and satiny smooth. Use tamper to help push ingredients down into blade. Only add a little coconut water if your having a hard time turning things over in blender. Push tamper quickly and forcefully down the inside of each curve in your blender. Filling should be thick, like consistency of mashed potatoes. Pour an inch of filling into pie crust. Place 2 layers of thin pineapple across filling then pour out remaining filling on top of pineapple. Spread top with small offset spatula or spoon to level and put in freezer for 25 minutes then refrigerator. Can decorate after flan hardens for half hour. When ready to serve release pie from spring form pan & place on plate.

Suggested toppings: Dried coconut, fresh fruit, edible flowers, raspberry syrup, chopped candied nuts, edible flowers   Edible Flowers pictured: Purslane & Dianthus

Ice Cream
(shown with Apple Raviolis from page 104)

2 cups soaked cashews
1 cup good water
2 tablespoons maple syrup
splash of vanilla

Put everything in blender but with half cup of the water. Blend on high till nuts are 80% creamed than add remaining water. Continue blending on high till satiny smooth, one minute. Pour into container and put in freezer for 40 minutes. Pour into ice cream maker and follow manufacturer's instructions.

SERVING SUGGESTIONS: Serve with a candied cacao nibs and dehydrated kiwi and pineapple slices.

Candied Cacao: mix some maple syrup with cacao nibs and dehydrate

Cara-mel Apples
Makes 4 medium apples

4 apples (Granny Smith, Golden Delicious or Jona Gold are best)
4 sticks
1 cup cashew butter
1/2 cup to 3/4 cup maple syrup
splash of vanilla
pinch of salt

Toppings
cacao nibs
orange segments
candied almonds
dehydrated raspberry
dried mulberries, dehydrated & finely minced

Wash apples but do not peel. Dry very well as caramel doesn't stick to moisture. Add butter, syrup, vanilla & salt to food processor. Turn on for 1 minute. If caramel is too thick drizzle a little more syrup. The more syrup the runnier caramel will be. The runnier the caramel the easier caramel will run down (fall off) your apple. Stick candy apple sticks in top center of your apple and dunk in caramel, turning quickly to coat. Place on a piece of wax paper containing candy apple toppings and roll apple until well coated. With a squeeze jar make designs over toppings with chocolate syrup and vanilla cream. Put in freezer for 30 minutes.

See video at CaraMelApples.com

The recipes contained in this book are the meals I've enjoyed throughout my adult life. These foods have nourished and perfected me for years as well as adding a much higher quality of life than any mainstream foodstuff can.
Living Proof of Living Foods :-)

See more recipe videos at MarkusNews.com

Other Life Changing Things from Us

See all kinds of videos, tips and recipes at MarkusNews.com

HEAL YOURSELF 101   The definitive book on self-healing and true health. This is the core book that started it all. It's easy to understand, gets right to the point and tells you literally how Markus turned his life around and never got sick again- no doctors, no pills. You can do this at home for almost nothing. Step by step. Includes recipes & diagrams. A worldwide bestseller. Sold 100,000 copies in Germany alone!
Paperback or ebook

HEAL YOUR FACE   Yes wrinkles can reverse. What we call "aging" is not normal. Unhappy with your face? Your body is telling you something. Every line, wrinkle, spot, mole and crease mean something. Every part of your face is connected to an organ or body part. If that body part is not functioning properly, it will show up on your face, teeth and hair. Forget plastic surgery- you can do it yourself.

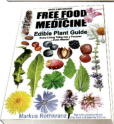

FREE FOOD AND MEDICINE WORLDWIDE EDIBLE PLANT GUIDE 480 pages
Over 2,500 beautiful full color illustrations of the most popular edible plants found all around the world, and what their health benefits are. Includes toxic plant recognition chart, how to harvest, different methods of preparation, specific health condition reference, how to grow your own, etc. There's no other book like this. 2 lbs but pocketsized No home should be without this amazing book. Eat your weeds!

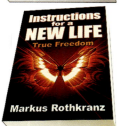

INSTRUCTIONS FOR A NEW LIFE The book we should have been given from the beginning. Possibly one of the most important life-changing books ever written. This is the definitive step-by-step book on starting over from a life of confusion, desperation, pain and emptiness. In a relationship, health or money prison? Don't waste one more minute of your life. What is the meaning of life? The answer is so simple it will change you forever.

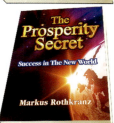

THE PROSPERITY SECRET This book should be mandatory reading. Success has nothing to do with the economy, other people, hard work, skill, talent or luck. The richest people get rich during hard times. Find out how. The world is depending on you knowing this! Get out of victim mode and take charge of your life.
Hardcover and 4 disk DVD set $49.97

Always Love.

INDEX

Almond nut crunch 88
Appetizers 110
Apple raviolis 104
Asian salad 80
Bacon, Jerky 34, 122
Bangkok Thai soup 64
Barley on the half shell 170
Bread 24, 184
Breakfast, American fun 120
Broccoli and cheese 194
Brotwurst spreadable sausage 108
Burger patty 28
Banana, mango "toast" 126
Cactus aloe smoothie 44
Candy Cara-mel apples 224
Canoli 204
Cashew vanilla milk 18
Cashew cream (savory) 18
Cashew cream (sweet) 18
Cheese 24, 74, 192
Cheese and crackers 206
Cheese, date, pineapple salad 74
Cheesecake 214
(un)Chicken Kung Pao 148
(un)Chicken noodle soup 66
(un)Chicken tacos 140
Chips for dips 96
Chocolate 90
Chocolate, almond, flax cookies 98
Chocolate crush pie 208
Chocolate dipped, almond cookies 102
Chocolate mousse 210
Chocolate milk 52
Chocolate smoothie 58
Chocolate syrup 36
Chocolate tacos 200
Cleansing breakfast 132
Coconut cream flan cake, with pineapple filling 220
Condiments 30
Cookies 103, 98
Cookies, chocolate dipped 102
Corn chowder soup 68
Cracker 36, 166,
Creme brûlée 198
Cream 18, 156
Crepe 212, 219

230

Creamy mashed potatoes, veggies and onion rings 32
Crispy "toast" cashew butter, mango and banana 126
Curry omelet 128
Curry noodle, Thai 162
Deli slices 26
Deserts 198, 200, 202, 204, 206, 208, 210, 212, 214, 216, 218, 220, 222, 224
Dried tomato poppers, with cheese and onion rings 92
Drinks 38
Durian custard with fruit 130
Endive hummus boats 112
Freezer chocolate, marzipan 90
Fruit cracker 36
Fruit cracker Deluxe 106
Fruit crepe 212
Fruit leather crepe 218
Fruit salad(s) 122
Garlic naan 24
Gourmet pizza 166
Grapefruit, garlic, ginger daydream 48
Greek salad 76
Green crunch salad 78
Green dream juice, lemongrass, ginger chuenchai 54
Green smoothie 40
Ice cream 202
Indian feast 152
Jalapeno poppers 116
Jerky 34
Kale salad by Markus 72
Ketchup 30
Kids 186, 188, 190, 192, 194
Kung Pau unChicken 148
Lasagna 180
Lunch 134
Lunch meat and chips 26
Macaroni and cheese 188
Mango, blueberry mint 158
Markus Incredipizza 182
Marzipan 90
Mayonnaise 30, 136
"Meat" 26, 28, 34, 66, 108, 120, 136, 138, 144, 148, 152, 178, 182, 184
Milk 18
Mint lime raspberry cocktail 46
Mustard 30
Mashed potatoes 32
Nigiri sushi 178
Noodle, spicy Thai curry unChicken 152
Noodle, Italian veggies 168

Nut Crunch 88
Oatmeal 124
Omelet 128
Onion rings 32, 92
Orange slices with protein powder 100
Pasta in cream sauce 154
Pasta pomodoro 160
"PBJ" jam and nut butter on "toast" 126
Pies 208, 214, 216, 220
Pina colada 60
Pink passion pie 216
Pizza 166, 172, 184
Pop tarts 190
Potato chips 94
Pumpkin parfait 56
Pumpkin raviolis 140
Relish 30
Reuben 144
Raspberry mint lime cocktail 46
Ravioli 104, 140
Rice 150, 178
Salads 70, 72, 74, 76, 78, 80, 82, 84
Salsa, tropical 164
Sea moss 20
Seaweed salad 82
Shiitake mushroom pizza 174
Smoothies 38, 40, 42, 44, 58
Snacks 86
Soups 64, 66, 68
Spaghettios 192
Spicy Thai cabbage 156
Spicy, Thai curry noodle unChicken 152
Spring rolls 114
Strawberry parfait 56
Strawberry smoothie 42
Sushi 174, 176, 178
Tabouli salad 84
Tacos 138
Thai spicy, curry noodle unChicken 152
Thai curry noodle 162
Thousand Island Dressing 144
Tropical salsa 164
(un)Tuna salad, mayonnaise 136
Vegetable vesuvio over noodles 168
Veggie juice 50
Wraps 142
Yogurt sauce 150